Ex Libris

The Cat's Whiskers

The Cat's

Whiskers

Beryl Reid
with the assistance of
Eric Braun

EBURY PRESS · LONDON

AUTHORS' ACKNOWLEDGEMENTS

The authors' thanks are gratefully due to all who contributed information or suggestions to *The Cat's Whiskers*, including permission to reprint extracts from the following: *The Song of Mehitabel* by Don Marquis, published by Faber and Faber and Penguin Books; *Cuisine for Cats* by Richard Graham, published by Pedigree Books; Joyce Wright's article on Dame Anna Neagle's cat Tuppence (Woman's Own Syndication Department); *There's Always Tomorrow* by Dame Anna Neagle (© Everest Films Ltd, 1974). For invaluable and often riveting research our thanks to Anne Johnson, *She Book of Cats* by Pamela Carmichael, published by Ebury Press, and to Faith Hines for her books on Dick Whittington.

Interviews and material were kindly given by Raye Virginia Allen, Eileen Atkins, Valerie Braithwaite, Muriel Carey, Roger Carne, Terri Howard, Eric Joyce, Robert Luff, Siân Phillips, Audrey Smith, Joan Wallace and Margaret Woodward.

Omitted due to lack of space were interesting stories and letters from numerous contributors, including Dorothy Burton, Jeanette Charles, Frances Cox, Connie Geary, Mark Haddon, Norman Holland, Anthea Holloway, Alan Martell and June Macy, W. Stanley Moore, Jill Racy, Archie Tappenden, Vicki Trew, Shirley Sutton, Sheila Sainsbury-Brown and Veronica Twiddle. Our regrets and thanks to everyone concerned.

Editor: Suzanne Webber
Art Director: Frank Phillips
Designer: Harry Green
Commissioned Photographs: Christopher Drew
Illustrations: David Parkins
Picture Research: Jan Croot

Published by Ebury Press
Division of The National Magazine Company Limited
Colquhoun House, 27–37 Broadwick Street
London W1V 1FR

First impression 1986
Second impression 1986
Copyright © 1986 by Strithon Ltd

ISBN: 0 85223 568 2

Photographic credits

Page 8 Terry Moore; 13 BBC; 18, 20 Associated Newspapers Group Limited; 21 Douglas H Jeffery; 22 Associated Newspapers Group Limited; 27 Topham; 31 Claudia Warner; 32 The Mansell Collection; 35, 36/37 Mary Evans Picture Library; 39 and 40 (left) Brewery Artists/Edwin C Peckham; 40 (right) Brewery Artists; 44/45 *Observer*/John Hawkins; 47 (top left) Rank Organisation; 47 (bottom) *Woman*; 54 The Mansell Collection; 56 (top) National Trust; 56 (bottom) The Illustrated London News Picture Library/Edward Arnold; 57 The Savoy; 59/63 (top) The Illustrated London News Picture Library/Edward Arnold; 63 (bottom) Glenturret Distillery Limited; 64 COI; 65 June Watson; 66 Mrs Gwladys Cooper/*South Wales Argus*; 70, 71, 72, 73 Topham; 93 United Press International (UK) Limited; 96 Joyce Wright; 99 Terry Moore; 103 John Roden; 106 Wm Edmund Barrett; 110 Amanda/Braithwaite Theatrical Agency.

Filmset and printed in Great Britain by BAS Printers Limited
Bound by Butler & Tanner Limited

Contents

Dedication

To all cats

*I love cats and I hope they feel the same
about me. Cats have struggled, sailed and
forced their way through history. They have
seen more ups and downs than any other
animals, being adored and detested alternately
for 10,000 years, but they, rather like me,
are survivors and refuse to be defeated or squashed
by anything. That is why we, who love them, still
continue to have the pleasure of their company.*

Preface

March 18 was a very important day for me, because I was going to go to Buckingham Palace to receive the OBE from the Queen. I got up very early—it was a bit of an effort, I'll have you know that—and the first thing to do, even before washing my face, was to feed ten cats, because they *do* come first. So, having fed the ten cats and stepped over ten tails, all lined up in the kitchen, I then started on myself and sketched in a face from memory. I wore a rather nice suit which was a dark apricot colour—a very becoming colour but one you don't see a lot of, though it's one of my favourites. I had a hat to match, but of course I'd forgotten that there were three roses at the back of the hat and I had to hold them over the kettle and shake them out to steam them, as I thought the Queen might see the top of my head! Then I set off.

I was going with Robert Luff, who has been my agent for longer than either of us cares to remember. He was standing by his Rolls, looking very handsome in his beautiful morning suit. It's a very old Rolls and rather hard to climb into, but still is the most beautiful thing in the world. We then drove to the Palace, where we were put in a kind of a pen, like a sheep pen (carpeted, of course) with a little rope round it, and we were separated into sections of people. I don't understand how the sections are chosen—it was

not alphabetical order or to do with the orders or medals we were going to get, but I was very lucky to be in about the fourth, because it does get boring, when there are a hundred and seventy-six honours being bestowed.

Everything was done in the most wonderful way. In the Minstrels' Gallery was a great big orchestra, playing the most lovely light music— selections from musicals like *My Fair Lady*. They didn't do one from *Gigi*, which I had been in at the time—I was sorry about that. It was all cheerful light music, played fairly loud, but the Queen never had to raise her voice, because there was a man standing there who announced everybody, each person and each honour as it came along. The Queen just spoke to you very gently as you went up and she pinned the Order on to you.

She said, 'How's the show going, and are you still managing to do it?' I said 'Actually, at the moment I'm not in it, because I have been rather ill.' She said, 'Well, it was really very energetic, wasn't it?', because she'd seen it at the Royal Variety Show, when I was going mad and doing the splits and all that sort of thing. We had a lovely conversation, because with her they always are, and when she sees somebody she knows her face absolutely lights up, because she must have to talk to so many people she doesn't know and magic words out of the air. I think that's the hardest thing. After I had been given the Award from the Queen, I then went out of another door, which you're told about in the beginning, when you're doing the drill, and did about eight interviews with press people. After that I was allowed back into the hall to watch a lot of other people being honoured for bravery and goodness knows what: the ceremony was all very exciting and done in such a relaxed sort of way that it was nearly like a party, though I must say there was only water in all the flasks about the place.

I watched a great deal of it, then we came out into the quadrangle, which is where you lose everybody, because you can't possibly locate cars or people; there are so many people, so many photos being taken. The professional photographer who was to take everybody's picture hadn't turned up, so when he finally did we had to queue again. Eventually I did find Robert Luff; I was gathered up and bundled into the Rolls again and we went to his club in Pall Mall, the RAC, as he was a major in the Gordon Highlanders, where we had an absolutely scrumptious lunch. We murdered a drink before we had it, because just going to the Palace had been nerve-wracking and trying, though it was relaxing when we got there.

Then he very sweetly drove me back to Honeypot Cottage on the Thames: he was *enamoured* of the cats—he loves cats—and in his splendid morning suit he played with the cats for an hour and a half on the lawn, kneeling on the wet green grass. Eventually I was left here to look at my OBE and feed the cats again, so it's a vicious circle, but it was a wonderful day and one I will never ever forget.

In The Beginning...

In the beginning at Honeypot Cottage there was Footy. Her birth was extraordinary, because her mother was wild (I eventually called her Ella, because she had a very sexy walk, like Ella Fitzgerald) and chose to have her kittens in the straw beside the water tank on my roof. I was married to Derek Franklin then, and we could hear this little crying noise, so we got up on to the roof, which you can by scaling the wall, and there were five tiny tiny kittens. We lifted them down, one at a time, and put them into the shed, which has now been made into an extra bedroom. Ella was not very well pleased about this, because we'd touched them, which was something I didn't realize about wild cats, so she came and killed them, one at a time, like Medea, whom my friend Eileen Atkins is playing at the time of writing. I took Footy, who was the most advanced kitten, into my house. For three months Ella kept looking for Footy to take her away but by that time she quite belonged to me.

She was called Footy because she always sat on my foot when I was in the kitchen doing some work, and I had to walk about with her on my foot. She was a magical cat, really—black, long-haired and without any malice at all, except for my brother Roy, which was

sleep together and love each other. Life is a bowl of cherries if there are two together, but if there's only one, that one takes all your attention and becomes very spoilt.

FOOTY AND FRED

Fred, too, was jet black and became very large. He grew to be 18 lbs. One day I heard Joan say to Fred, 'Come on, Freddie—in the bathroom with me; I'll carry you!' I said 'No wonder he's that size, Joan, because he never walks anywhere' and the vet once said, 'Underneath all that fat, there is a cat!'

Footy and Fred were lovely all their lives, but especially when they were kittens. I had a big orange straw sun hat, and my mother was staying with me on one occasion when we watched this straw hat walk across the room with eight legs which, of course belonged to Footy and Fred. I must say they gave me a million laughs. Footy was quite extraordinary; she was always the one who waited for me on the first bridge when I came home from the theatre at night. She was uncanny: I went to Cornwall for four days to do some surfing. I rang Joan every day to ask if the cats were all right. One day she said, 'Oh, yes, yes—they're fine.' I said, 'Joan, that means they're not, when it's that voice.' She said, 'Well, I can't find Footy.' Footy came home an hour before I came home on the fourth day, because she knew that I was away; she must have come in through the cat flap when Joan wasn't here and eaten things, but she would not appear to anybody until I came home.

something I never understood. When my brother came to visit me, which was something I used to look forward to very much, she used to march smartly across the room and bite him—why, I never could fathom because he was a quiet and gentle person. So I thought she must be rather lonely and acquired another little kitten whom I called Fred.

Carol, who was the youngest daughter of my dear friend Joan Bissett, who worked for me for twenty happy years, had heard that there was an unwanted kitten at a fish farm quite near home, and I thought that this would be a lovely friend for Footy—it's so much easier to have two cats than it is to have one. I strongly advise anyone who is going to have a kitten— 'We're going to have a kitten,' they say—not to have 'a kitten' but to have two, because they look after each other, play with each other,

One thing about Footy, which I think dated back to her leaving her mother so very early, was that she never learned to clean herself. This is something I thought they did perfectly naturally, but apparently they don't; their mothers teach them to do it, and because she was taken away from Ella so early in life she never learned to get cracking with her tongue. Being long-haired she did get very

at all, it was just a sort of trick that they do. She performed another neat trick once when Jimmy Edwards came to dinner, and I'd cooked a turkey. I love him, but he was sort of silly, because he'd let two Jack Russell terriers out of the car, forgetting, or not wishing to remember, that I'd got cats. They tore after Footy as soon as they saw her and gave chase like bats out of hell. 'I'll never see her again,

Being long-haired she did get very knotted knickers and so the vet had to come every now and then and de-knot her.

knotted knickers and because I was such a coward about it the knots were allowed to get quite big so the vet had to come every now and then and de-knot her, which of course can't be very pleasant. Once when the vet came to do the de-knotting, Footy hated it so much that she ran away from home when he'd gone—she left every now and then, because she was very strong-willed. I was calling out, 'Footy, Footy, wherever you are, I love you!' and I'd not noticed that in the meantime the milkman had come with the milk. He just handed me the two bottles of milk and ran for his life, thinking he'd got an absolute madwoman on his hands!

When she was tiny Footy spent a terrible night—for me—up a tree which was over the river. I thought she couldn't get down and at five o'clock in the morning I was up this tree, desperately trying to get her down, but she suddenly turned and just walked down quite calmly behind me. She had never been stuck

never see her again—Jimmy, you are so silly!' I said and stood crying for ten minutes, 'you shouldn't have let them out of the car—you shouldn't do that to me,' while he said, 'Oh, don't be silly, of course she'll come back,' rather nervously, I must say. Suddenly they came back into vision, in reverse order, with Footy chasing the two Jack Russells! She was really proving that she was very game.

After this about-face Jimmy settled down to enjoy himself; he was obviously having rather a good time—a few drinks and things, and we were eating the turkey. He'd had a leg and part of the breast, then he said, 'Can I have another leg?' and I said, 'Yes, all right.' He soon dealt with that, then he said, 'Can I have another leg?' I said, 'The poor beast's only got two, Jimmy!' It proved to be an enjoyable evening after the dogs had been put back into the car with Footy walking about very proudly, her tail pointing straight to heaven.

1962: Rehearsing The Merry Wives of Windsor *with
'Big Jim' (Jimmy Edwards) and producer Cedric Messina*

She was an adorable cat—a witches' cat. When I did Noel Coward's play *Blithe Spirit* and was acting the part of a medium, Madame Arcati (who could be said to have been more than a little bit eccentric), I had a great number of letters from spiritualist societies to persuade me to join them. I thought I was just acting out what I was told to do, but obviously they thought there was much more to it and, as it turned out, the most extraordinary things did happen to me. I must have been angering somebody, or provoking some spiritual force. At one time Footy was 'lost'. She had been missing for forty-eight hours and I was getting rather nerve-wracked about it. I had just done a television interview with Michael Parkinson, who had been extremely nice to me, but I felt very much on edge because I hadn't found Footy. My brother Roy was with me at the time and my sister-in-law Pat, was also staying with me. We came back and were having cold steak and kidney pie—for some reason 'I Remember

It Well'!—and I'd just dished it up and showed them the salad and baked potato that went with it, when I jumped up from the table and said, 'Oh, she's beside the water tank where she was born!' There is a ladder, absolutely level with the wall, which goes up to my roof, and I shinned up this ladder, still wearing my mink jacket and a long dress, but couldn't lift the lid off the watertank as I'd got a bit grander then and had had a roof put on it. I thought to myself, 'I've just got to, as there's not room for me *and* Roy on the ladder.' I heaved the lid with all my strength and out popped Footy. Of course that's where she had been all the time.

At around the same time other extraordinary things did happen to me. I had a little tiny mirror on my dressing table. It was winter sunlight—that lovely pale yellow cold sunlight that you sometimes get in the winter, with no heat in it whatsoever—and suddenly my bedroom curtains were on fire, which seems extraordinary, so I really must have been annoying somebody, a little poltergeist or something that was *not* well pleased with what I did.

Then I went and stayed in my friend Jack Tripp's house in Brighton while he was away. It was such a beautiful and grand house that I used to sit well away from everything, because I felt I was destruction on legs. I sat right at the end of the room and all of a sudden all his curtains fell down. It was a bay window and there was no hope of my even getting them off the ground.

On another occasion I was driving along in my car and I suddenly realized I'd left the leather case with all my keys, except the car key, behind and I had to go back to the parade of shops in Langley, all of which I had visited. Then suddenly something said in my head, 'Why don't you look in your umbrella?' I never use an umbrella. I know there's one in the boot of my car, but I never actually put up an umbrella because it's just a waste of time. I either poke somebody in the eye, or fall over it or lose it or something, so it just sits in the boot of my car. But still—'Why don't you look in your umbrella?' I pulled in to the side of the road, stopped the car, opened the boot and there were all my keys—can you guess?—in my umbrella.

Fred came into his own in a big way shortly before I went to South Africa to appear in a revue called *Something New* with John Boulter, not the one from *The Black and White Minstrel Show*, but a talented young man who was one of South Africa's most popular players and who became a good friend. The press came to photograph me packing for the trip, with Footy and Fred 'helping' me by unravelling balls of wool and suchlike. When the picture appeared in the papers it was captioned 'Fred (left) and Footy help Beryl to pack for her journey.' It quite went to Fred's head and I don't think he ever got over the sudden rush of fame.

Footy lived a great long life, at least eighteen years, and Fred to seventeen and a half. They were my first two cats at Honeypot Cottage, although Ella did try to overrun the place with more, because she felt she could trust me, which I'm afraid I betrayed. Whenever she had kittens she brought them across the stream and put them in the centre of a big willow tree like a nest, so that I should take care of them, but as they were all interbred—at one time there were thirty—I had to get them rounded up by the RSPCA and put to sleep. I could not feed or look after so many properly. The kindest thing in the world is to have a cat, male or female, neutered, because there are so many unwanted cats in the world. As I do so much work for the RSPCA, I feel most strongly that if only people had the sense to have them neutered the cat population would be so much happier and so much healthier. Cats are just left in cardboard boxes, they're dumped and some have terrible lives. It's a nonsense that cats must have a litter before they're neutered because what you've never had you never miss. That goes for dogs too—before the time comes for them to be in season, grovelling about and unhappy. The idea that they should have a litter is a myth—a pure old wives' tale, and if someone can't afford to have a cat neutered in Britain, the RSPCA will give financial help because that is what the RSPCA are for— caring for animals and giving them better lives. I feel very very strongly about it; my ten are all neutered and therefore not a nuisance.

CHILDHOOD CATS

But, back to the beginning of my life—pre-Honeypot: (P.H.)—which, for me is almost equal to B.C. When I was little I had one cat called Jumbo, who was all black like Footy and Fred, funnily enough. I had a traumatic week at the Argyll Theatre, Birkenhead, when I was having a very tough time because I was the first turn and was getting The Bird. My brother came to take me home every night and on the Saturday night when I had packed up to go (having stuck the week out with great difficulty, being paid a paltry £5), he came to tell me that Jumbo had been killed on the railway lines. I was dotty about Jumbo, and we'd had a happy life together, so it was rather upsetting for Roy to have to bring me the news as the climax to such a horrible week.

Then there was Hamish, which is Gaelic for John, because my mother was from Edinburgh and thought Hamish was a lovely name. He was also all-black: it seems that my life then featured just the Black Minstrels, not the Black and White ones. If Mummy had gone to bed I had to get Hamish in, because we hadn't got a cat flap then, because we didn't go in for cats in a big way—we just had one cat, like people used to have. I had to go to the back door and clap my hands and sound like my mother and say, 'Come along, Hamish—that's the Boy— Come along—that's the Boy!' I thought this was exactly like my mother and I looked up at the tall railing we had along the path at the side of the house and Hamish was sitting, looking down at me contemptuously, as if to say, 'Do you really think that's like my mother? Because it's not at all!'

In those far-off days when I was 12, I had the first of my tortoises, Matthew I. I had great fondness for those little creatures, and during my first marriage, to Bill Worsley, Matthew II came into my life, at our homes in Amersham and Sunbury-on-Thames. This was, of course, all 'P.H.'. At Honeypot Cottage, Jean and Arthur were the resident tortoises, and they spent eight happy years here, in their own little houses, with chimneys and doors.

Like some of the cats, they were inclined to stray and to become 'what is called 'LOST'. Once they made their way to my near neighbour, Miss Pugh, a real animal lover, who not only returned them, wading across the stream in her Wellingtons, but had put them snugly in a box with straw and lettuce leaves in case they got hungry on the journey!

Since then it has been realized that these endearing small reptiles are not happy over here: they become confused by the weather—a warm day in the middle of a cold spell makes them think it's time to come out of hibernation and they try to walk about and use energy they need to store up. They are no longer imported as pets, because it is now recognized that they are far better off in the tropical climates where they originated.

Footy really set me on the path to becoming a great cat lover. Just as events happen in people's lives, cats happen to me: I've had a trail of them ever since. My grandfather on my mother's side used to have a few drinks and take all the stray cats home with him, and I think that must be a throw-back for me. It was an extraordinary thing that *he* attracted cats and they seem to appear in *my* life. I never look for them; they just happen. It's rather like Colette, who wrote *Gigi*; she was besotted with cats and used to make friends with them all over the world. She was in England, having great trouble with the language when she saw two cats on the wall. She had a long conversation with them in French and said to a woman, 'There you are—you see, they are the only people who understand French!'

Cats And The Theatre

For many years it was considered very lucky to have cats in the theatre. In my own story the first with whom I made friends lived at the Gaiety, Ayr, when I was there in a lovely season of *The Gaiety Whirl* with one of my favourite people, the Scots comic genius Dave Willis. Cuppy, the theatre cat who walked into my life as a little kitten, was so christened because he used to do the rounds backstage on the shoulder of Archie the stage doorkeeper. He was called Cuppy because he took to following me everywhere like a puppy. He had other unusual talents, like the letter he wrote to my brother Roy when he was ill with a duodenal ulcer. I make no apology for quoting Cuppy in full.

Dear Roy,

I believe you have a duodenal ulcer. You are very lucky—I only have a cork on the end of a string to play with. I have a lovely time here, except that people rub my head too much. When I get fed up with this I go to sleep in a hole in the wall which is the same colour as me, and then I am what is called 'lost'. Everybody shouts for me and I take no notice at all, and then, later on when I've slept for long enough, and people shout again, Beryl comes along, looking desperate, saying 'Have you seen my cat'— *as I think she calls me—I get up and stretch and everybody rubs my head wildly again, and I am what is called 'found'.*

Love Cuppy

Beerbohm,
lord of the
Globe

Cuppy fooled people in other ways for years. I thought 'he' was a boy but it turned out she was a girl when, after a lost weekend—hers, not mine— just before I left Ayr, she went off to live with my Auntie Belle and presented her with kittens and they all enjoyed the rest of their lives in her little cottage in the country.

BEERBOHM AND BOSS-CAT

All these years later it's still very lucky to have cats in the theatre. More than thirty years after Cuppy, I met Beerbohm when I did *Born In The Gardens* at the Globe. Named after the great actor-manager Sir Beerbohm Tree, he lives at the Globe in great splendour. He has a jewelled collar and while I was playing there they made him a lovely house in the prop room, where all the stage hands go, with *Born In The Gardens* written on the front of his house. He was a beautiful little cat and was sort of heart-broken at the end of the show and sat on every basket (at the end of runs they pack all the clothes up in hampers, which are then shipped off to some storage place and kept there). Beerbohm would not get off the baskets—he wanted to go in every one, which was terribly sad for me to watch. But he still reigns supreme there.

Mind you, he did have some rather dicey friends, who belonged to the market people. Boss-cat was barred from the theatre because he thought it was a sort of up-market loo: living as he did among a lot of vegetable boxes, he thought to come into the theatre and have a great big jolly mess and a wee really rather swinging. The doorkeeper Brendan, one of my

Boss-cat was barred from the theatre because he thought it was a sort of up-market loo.

dearest friends, with whom I've kept in constant touch by telephone, though I haven't even been along to see him yet, said, 'No, I've barred him the theatre—I've barred him the theatre. I won't let him in!' Boss-cat was adorable and about twice the size of Fred. He was an enormous cat and lived on one of the vegetable stalls with Cheeky and Blackie, who were also market cats.

FLEUR

At the Lyric, where I have recently been playing, was Fleur. She was a scrap of a little thing when I arrived at the theatre, but since I

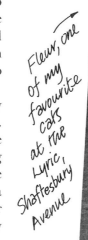

Fleur, one of my favourite cats at the Lyric, Shaftesbury Avenue

opened there in August she has blossomed and is now really a very beautiful little cat, although she was run over at one time and so her back leg is lame. I would dearly like to have her living out her retirement at Honeypot Cottage.

THEATRE CATS OF THE PAST

Theatre cats lived in the theatre just to keep things shipshape and Bristol-fashion and this included keeping the rodents at bay. The position is illustrated by T. S. Eliot: his cat was called Gus—an abbreviation of Asparagus. He used to sit at the theatre stage door and was 'elderly and thin as a rake', but the poet-playwright of *Murder In The Cathedral* and *The Cocktail Party* insisted that nobody could trifle with him: he was a very severe cat, aware of his status as Minder for one of the geniuses of the theatre.

Famous theatre cats of the past almost justify a *Who's Who* of their own. Bouncer lived

I wonder what he thinks of it

Elaine Paige as Grisabella

very exciting experience in the theatre, but to me a disappointment, because the Cats look as though they've been skinned. They wear skin-tight leotards with paint sprayed on them and leg-warmers and I feel that Gillian Lynne, the director-choreographer, whom I admire so much, cannot have lived with cats, because the movement, in my opinion, has nothing to do with the way that cats really move. Occasionally you have glimpses of it: Grisabella, the scraggy, passée, sexy cat, played by Elaine Paige when I saw the show, put her feet down in the right way. It was a most moving scene when she's about to die and walks up a staircase into the sky. I must say that Elaine Paige really made me conscious that the musical was really about cats, and Brian Blessed as Deuteronomy, the king of this tip they live on, sits there singing so marvellously really looking like a king-cat. Who am I to say that the cats in this spectacle, and are of the greatest theatrical successes in the world, don't look like cats?—it's only that I've lived very closely with cats for such a long time and was disappointed not only that they didn't move more like cats but that there was no peace in the show. Cats are very relaxing peaceful creatures and anyone who lives with cats and watches them relax never has high blood pressure or any heart condition—I'm filled with envy sometimes, when I'm jumpy or trying to learn something or do something, because they have the most *perfect* form of relaxation. I have four cats on my bed as I'm saying this.

But, to get back to theatre cats of the past, Plug at the Adelphi was another very serious-

at the Garrick Theatre, a beautiful imposing silver-grey tabby who transferred to the Fortune about seven years ago. He had his own apartment, cat-wise, on the fifth floor and when a new management took over some two years later he left with his friend the manageress to share her home away from the theatre: he is still flourishing and no doubt growing fat on the shares which he still owns in the musical *Cats*! I found this a wonderful spectacle and a

Ambrose, Guardian of the Upper Circle

minded cat, who used to patrol the stalls with his sister, Socket: he was black with white paws and both of them used to attend the rehearsals, but never the shows. They didn't like it when the show had opened, but they enjoyed the rehearsals and seeing the actors gradually improve.

Then there was Ambrose at The Drury Lane Theatre: he looked from a distance as if he was wearing evening-dress—a black jacket with an immaculate white shirt front. During *A Chorus Line* he decided to walk coolly across the stage to a round of applause. He died, unfortunately, in August 1985 and the theatre has no plans to replace him.

Cats are irreplaceable, as I've always said, having had a tremendous number of them: you don't ever replace a cat or a person, but you find another place in your heart for the next one who enters your life. They have their own place in your heart, but you can never replace cats, dogs or people.

At the Aldwych Theatre there was a black half-Persian with green eyes who was reputed to receive as much fan mail as any actor: I find that very hard to believe, but maybe the actors were very bad and didn't get much fan mail!

Cats on stage have, in the main, confined themselves to spectacular walk-ons—even walk-throughs—although long ago at the Folies Bergères in Paris they had an animal act. I must say that they've had some very funny animals on display there in the form of feathers behind ladies, or ladies behind feathers, (not to mention fruit in the shape of bananas strategically placed both in front of and behind Josephine Baker), but the act in question included monkeys and a cat whose performance consisted of leaping through a hoop to balance herself prettily on a large rubber ball,

of course it was, because he had so many successes in his lifetime.

Another great name to be given a large share of luck by a theatre cat at a First Performance, this time in London, was Paderewski when he gave his piano concert at the St. James Theatre in 1890. He saw the cat sitting in full view of the audience as he walked on and he said, 'Wish me luck, won't you,' whereupon the animal jumped upon his lap and purred—in concert pitch, mind you, they're not daft—until the end of the first selection. The concert was a great success and afterwards Paderewski played to invited guests in the green room, which is where actors sit backstage and talk to each other over cups of coffee or whatever. He played, naturally, Scarlatti's *Cat Fugue*, which was a piece inspired by the composer's cat

He walked across the stage in the middle of the thunderstorm, then coolly settled himself on an imitation boulder.

where she composed herself for sleep—if she was in the mood. If not, she would not appear at all, and was inclined to send on her understudy, if she was not out strutting her stuff on the Boulevards. Another cat to distinguish himself on a boulder, only on this occasion unrehearsed, was the one who appeared on stage in New York, during Sir Henry Irving's first performance of *Faust*. He walked across the stage in the middle of the thunderstorm, then coolly settled himself on an imitation boulder, which the actor-manager took as a good omen;

walking on the keys of the piano. Classical music has always sounded like that to me, anyway, but then I'm not a terribly musical person.

At the disastrous first performance of Rossini's *Barber of Seville* a cat walked on stage, turning the boos into laughter and bringing down both the house and the curtain. Considering the opera's lasting success ever since, he was another cat to bring good luck to the theatre: you see, these cats have featured very heavily in the arts.

CATS AT THE CONNAUGHT

Eric Joyce, the distinguished critic for the *Worthing Gazette* and *The Stage* among other papers, recently wrote to me about cats at the Connaught Theatre, with which he has been associated for over 30 years. I myself played there very happily in two productions in the late fifties for Melville Gillam, who is sadly no longer with us any more. They were both new plays, which gave me early opportunities to extend my acting experience in the straight theatre, for which I was very grateful. One was *The Dreamhouse* in which I was a fortune teller with Bill Owen. The other was *Witch Errant* in which I played the title part, and very eccentric she was too. Eric Joyce writes of his Connaught memories: 'Among the incidental tasks was the search for suitable pets to meet current production needs, the most demanding being the 'auditioning' of a Siamese cat to play Pyewacket in *Bell, Book and Candle*. On one occasion I remember, the Connaught's then leading lady, Anne Berry, and I spent the best part of a day interviewing the owners of possible candidates for the role.

Most were far too temperamental, while others were completely indifferent to the whole idea, then it was that we happened to chance on a likely lad with all the necessary qualifications. His mistress, while overjoyed at seeing her cat on stage, insisted that he could only make his Connaught début on one condition, that his brother go too. No amount of reasoning could persuade the good lady to change her mind, until it was suggested that one cat would be accepted for the part while the other would be on hand as understudy. She was quite happy with this arrangement and just one Pyewacket appeared on stage, while his lookalike brother remained in the wings awaiting the call to stardom.

As for Mac, the Connaught cat, the theatre seemed to enjoy a period of relative prosperity while he was in residence, its worsening fortunes coinciding with his mysterious departure. Now that plans are afoot for the theatre's reopening I must see that the Connaught starts off on the right foot by having a cat on the premises . . . a theatre without a cat is really unthinkable!

Hear, hear! And my love and good wishes always to the Connaught Theatre.

CAT AND MOONCAT

One of the things which touched my heart very much in *Breakfast At Tiffany's*, which is one of my favourite films, was the cat called Cat, which I thought was a most moving performance and made these extraordinary people, or rather these extraordinary characters in the story, seem so very touching and human, and that, I think, apart from the beauty and talent of Audrey Hepburn and the other actors, was entirely Cat's fault.

I worked with another very special cat, the puppet called Mooncat, who was green. I did eighty-two programmes for children at Yorkshire Television, called *Get Up And Go*, and, of course, it was carefully over-looked by the Education Authorities, so everything that I taught Mooncat had to be exactly right, like manners or cooking, or pounds, shillings and ounces. I was used to working with puppets, right back to my days with Peter Brough and Archie Andrews, so I didn't find it strange talking to a big green cat. They did the most amazing

> *I was used to working with puppets, so I didn't find it strange talking to a big green cat.*

technical feats with Mooncat, who was played by an extremely clever man called David Claridge, and a quite new audience appeared in my life through the series. While I was doing 'Mooncat', I opened a cat show in Birmingham and signed autographs for three hours (that isn't vanity, just necessity), and when I looked at the people there they ranged from two years old to eighty. I thought this is what you could really call cornering the market.

A wonderful little girl, who was being carried by her father, said 'Where's Mooncat?' I said, 'Well, you know he's green', and she said, 'Yes.' 'Well,' I said, 'he got fed up with being green, so he decided to be blue. He's changed himself into blue and it doesn't suit him at all— his eyes look all funny, so he's trying to turn himself back into green, but at the moment he's spotted, so that's why I couldn't bring him.' 'Oh, I *see*,' she said. 'Mooncat' was a wonderful link for me with children and I used to tell

Mooncat a story every week, which were published in a little book called *Here Comes Mrs. Pinkerton Trunks*. She, of course, was an elephant and there was also a little girl called Billie, a lion called Mr. Milford-Haven, a tiny little monkey called Monkey and other lovely characters. These stories that Mooncat used to listen to open-mouthed were written by Shirley Isherwood and these beautiful animals that had been so cleverly designed and embroidered, made a very entertaining and educational programme for children. So that was how I got my new little audience.

The older people at the show, of course,, had seen me in *Educating Archie, Entertaining Mr. Sloane, The Killing of Sister George.*

The only time I appeared 'purposely' with a real cat was when I did a Television programme discussing cat books called *The Practical Book Review.* I said I thought the most sensible book and the easiest to understand and most practical for anyone who has not kept a cat before was the one by the RSPCA, which was also the simplest to grasp. Then I did have a cat to hold and to 'act' with.

CAT SHOWS AND ROGAN THE PSYCHIC CAT

On another occasion I judged the cat competition with Brian Blessed at the Hilton (though I think he's more of a dog-lover really). There was a wonderful cat there whose mistress said he was psychic—Rogan, I think his name was— and I keep getting messages from her about how well he's doing and how well he's looking into people's futures and things like that. I would have found this hard to believe if I hadn't actually met the cat or its mistress. 'Quien sabe?' as Madame Arcati used to say. Anyway Rogan is a beautiful cat.

I must say I don't really like cat shows, as I don't like the idea of subjecting cats to all the discomfort and difficulty. They're all shut up in little boxes and it gets very very hot in these places with thousands of them crowded together, and they all sleep on their litter trays to try and keep cool. In fact I don't think it's right to exhibit any pet at all, because a great deal of discomfort goes with it: quite often the people leave them at the show all day and go out shopping in their cars and the cats get far too hot, they get tired, they get ratty and hungry, they wonder if they're going to go home— and I don't think it's a good thing. In fact, none of mine would get off their seats and go; they're a lazy lot, mine. I must say sometimes when I see an advertisement with a ginger cat in it I think Ronnie's gone out on his own and done it, but I never reap the reward for that!

CATS IN ADS

I'm not keen on advertising animals, either: I see my cats eat every day, sometimes four times a day, and they do not gollop food down (unless they have been kept without it for some time) as all these performing animals who appear in advertisements do—*they* wolf it down although cats are normally very dainty eaters. I don't think making them do that can be all that kind or that making money out of your animals is

a good thing to do, because they're going to pay for it in the long run, and I strongly advise against it.

A case in point is Arthur, probably one of the most famous television stars, who ate his cat food not just off a saucer like normal cats do— he scooped it out of a tin and licked it off his paw, and really was a great success on television commercials. Spillers signed him up in 1968 to advertise Kattomeat and that was when all the trouble started, because Spillers claimed that they had bought Arthur outright from an actor called Tony Manning, but he protested that the cat had only been rented. The court ruled in favour of Spillers, but Manning refused to hand Arthur over and was sent to jail for contempt of court. Manning demanded damages from Spillers, saying that they had caused some of Arthur's teeth to be extracted in order to encourage him to lick their product from his paw. The judge examined Arthur's four remaining teeth, tickled the cat under the chin, pronounced Manning to be 'an unscrupulous liar' and awarded Arthur to Kattomeat—not only a puzzling verdict, but a sad and upsetting tale. Arthur died on March 1st 1975, a month short of his seventeenth birthday, having featured in TV ads for eighteen weeks yearly and also having appeared in thirty-five films. I really hope he enjoyed his work, but feel his story could be a warning to echo Noel Coward's song, 'Don't put your pussy on the stage, Mrs. Worthington'!

Clever Clogs

CAN CATS ACT?

I think cats are natural show-offs, but I don't think they're natural actors, and I don't think they're nearly as easy to train as dogs are, because dogs are much more subservient than cats. However, I had a litter of three—Muriel, Sir Harry and Dimly, of whom more later— and when they were kittens they used to go into their little bedroom in the evening, because they were brought up in the spare room. We had a little drill, you see, and I got them all to jump up on to the bed and I stood and faced them and said, 'Sit!' and 'Stay!' and then I could turn away from them and go to the door and I used to say, 'I love you—see you tomorrow, and mind the bugs don't bite!' before putting off the light. I told Barbara Woodhouse about this and she said, 'I don't think you can *possibly* do that with cats.' I said, 'Well, *I* can,' I also trained the twins Paris and Tufnell, and although I couldn't teach them to sit, I did teach them, 'Stay!' Now, if there's something

Part of the Beryl bunch (from back to front): Muriel, Sir Harry, Tufnell and Dimly

awful going on—they're the newest ones and at the time of writing only nine months old— when told to stay, they stay.

Funnily enough, when Dimly got caught in a trap and had eleven stitches, he had to go back into the spare room to recover when he was about eighteen months old and he remembered everything that he had learned when he was in there: he sat and he stayed and he did all these little things he'd done before for me. But training cats like this needs sheer perseverance, and I don't think that cats are really meant to act, whereas dogs are.

I was doing the *Adrian Mole* television programmes and there was this wonderful quite scruffy-looking dog called Dog in the series. His master was demented about him and there was not an atom of cruelty in the way he trained him. Dog never looked subdued or anything and did everything he was told to do with such glee, and when he did a scene or anything else particularly well there was always a reward, which is something that dogs understand and cats don't. A little piece of chicken or some other treat from the food van was always accepted with joy and Dog was absolutely marvellous. The only trouble was that I'd broken my arm a few months before, and it had taken a very long time to get better so when the director Peter Sasdy told me to 'lift the dog across the road', I tried but the dog was about as big as me and I had great difficulty. Of course the way I found it easy to hold the dog the owner wouldn't let me do, because he said it wasn't comfortable for the Dog! I appreciated all that sort of thing and it was an adorable

dog. There was a lovely scene when Dog had been lost—it was kept on a piece of string and was always getting lost, because nobody took any notice of it and it acted that part very well because everybody was so fond of it—and I went and told Adrian, 'I've had this dog eight days, you know, Adrian, eight days. I thought somebody would have come round or written a letter or telephoned or something like that, but no—I've had this dog eight days and in eight days I could have run off with a Chinaman!' He said, 'But you don't know any Chinamen,' and I said 'In eight days I could have met, married and divorced one!' After that we heard Adrian's voice-over commenting in his diary, 'I've never seen a dog age so much in eight days, but then Grandma is very strict!'

In America, of course, they have something called Patsy Awards, which are animal equivalents of the Oscars, presented by the American Humane Association for the best animal performance in a film. I'm not surprised to find that Audrey Hepburn's Cat, whose real name was Orangey, won on two separate occasions, for *Breakfast At Tiffany*'s in 1962, and ten years before that for playing the title role in *Rhubarb*. So maybe I'm wrong about the talents of that cat at least. And it's fascinating to learn that the late Ethel Barrymore, who never went to see her own films, broke that rule once in 1948 when she went to see *Night Song*, in which her own silver tabby had played the part of her cat in the drama.

Well, every rule has its exceptions, but I still hold to my belief that cats are better off doing their own thing—within reason!

Cats
Of
The Past

I n my house you have to talk to cats because, being ten of them, there are a lot of important things you have to say to them—like 'Get off' and 'Shut up' and things like that. I've got one of them now on the bed where, as Mae West was so fond of saying, 'I do all my best work', that's purring so loudly that it could be heard in Africa. This is Jenny, whom I got from an old lady who was very interested in history and she must have heard me say to Eric, who's helping with this book, 'We're going to go back though the ages now.' I think Jenny's quite looking forward to the trip down memory lane, having lived so much in the past with her previous owner. Jenny has become quite set in her ways, being used to scraps from the old lady's food, so that is what she cares for most now, unlike the others. They're all so individual, you know, like people.

But 'I digress' as Marlene of the Midlands would say. I *do* talk to my cats and I find they respond: I don't think they understand what I say, but they certainly understand the tone of voice you use when you talk to them. They know when you're being very loving to them and very affectionate—otherwise why do they roll over? I mean, normally they don't roll over. I have two that come to the loo with me all the time and I only have to address them and they roll over. Mind you, I did once have a budgerigar—he was a tiny baby little thing and I thought he'd never learn to talk, because every time I addressed him he stood on his head in the seed box. His name was Humdummock and I thought he was never going to hear what I say, but eventually he did get over this tremendous excitement of being addressed and managed to say quite a lot to me.

I'm sure my cats would like to say quite a lot to me, but they have many ways of expressing themselves. Ronnie, who is named after Ronnie Corbett, touches me with his paw if he wants something very special, or attention, or a cuddle or something like that. But, if I raise my voice at all or speak to any of the cats in a severe sort of way they immediately stop what they're not supposed to be doing. The tone of your voice, particularly, is so very important.

The Two Ronnies, my favourite duo

The Goddess Bast (1789 BC to c AD 392). Also know as Pasht, from which 'Puss' might have derived. Note her elegant kit and the charming and alert kittens at her feet.

If it's soft talk or encouraging talk or getting them to take a pill or to eat something—all that you have to have to a fine art, really, and never think it's silly. I never think it's silly to talk to animals. A lot of people talk to plants, but I haven't got to that yet, and I'm sure my cats benefit considerably from my having conversations with them. I don't think they really know what the words mean—it's purely tone they go by, so it's just my little bit of fun about Jenny and her 'historical' background.

But she's purring even louder, so here goes. I must say I'm absolutely riveted reading and learning about cats in history, who really have had a Big Dipper up-and-down sort of existence through the ages. Like people they've been badly treated, they've been well treated, they've been abominably treated, but that goes for people too. The earliest known members of the small cat family made their first appearance on earth about 13,000 years ago, and it took another 10,000 years for the big cats to appear, like lions, tigers, leopards and the lynx. I find them all very beautiful indeed to look at. Perhaps I should have been a lion tamer—I don't know. Cats have been domesticated for 5,000 years, or perhaps even less, but dogs for 10,000, which I must say rather surprises me.

EGYPTIAN CATS

In ancient Egypt there was a cat-goddess called Pasht, who had the head of a cat, and she was worshipped in her temple at Bubastis. Actually, her real name was Bast, pronounced Pasht, from which it is said the word Puss came—I don't know, but anyway her statue sits in the British Museum, with a pleasant smile on her face and a couple of charming and alert kittens at her feet, waiting for offerings which never come. She had a good innings for a goddess, as she was worshipped on the lower Nile from at least 1780 BC to about AD 392. Her cats in the sacred temple are said to have had special guardians—Minders, as we might call them now—whose duty was to watch them constantly for any sign of a communication from the goddess.

Egyptian cats were very highly thought of—they were almost worshipped and the Sun God Ra was believed to turn into a cat every day at dawn to drive away the night by killing Apep, the serpent of darkness. When a cat died the family it lived with went into mourning and shaved their eyebrows—why their eyebrows I don't know, but they did—and when a house caught fire it was more important to save the household cat than any of the household goods. Killing a cat was punishable by death, because they were identified with Ra—no wonder, because any one of them could have been the Sun God in his daylight form, which makes it less than surprising that he was, in fact, Pasht's father.

The Egyptians believed that cats' eyes caught the fire of the sun by day and reflected it back at night, which meant that the sun would return the next morning, after Ra had done his stuff with Apep. That's rather a nice thought and must have inspired the man who invented cats eyes. If a cat was killed, the solar and lunar gods—the sun or moon gods—would

be angry and eternal darkness was threatened. Not only were cats, like their owners, mummified after death, but also mice, to provide the food for the cat in afterlife. The image of the cat was used to decorate jewellery and art: cats themselves were depicted wearing earrings and necklaces—all the precious stones available. Perhaps Beerbohm at the Globe was a throwback to this golden age of the cat!

On one occasion an Egptian town was beseiged by the Persians and the Persian commander ordered live cats to be thrown over the city walls, knowing that the defenders would rather surrender their city than risk injury to the cats. That was a good bit of their lives.

CHINESE AND JAPANESE CATS

Like the Egyptians the Chinese had lovely onomatopoeic words to label the cat: *miu* in Egyptian and *mao* in Chinese. In China cats have always been considered good luck and figured in their astrology and, like the Egyptians, the Chinese considered their eyes to have special powers. This made it not so pleasant for at least one household cat per family, which would be collared and chained so it could not roam away at night when its protection was most needed, to discourage and repel evil spirits with the gleam of its eyes. It was from China that cats were introduced into Japan in the tenth century. The first litter of kittens to be born in Japan were born in the Imperial Palace of Kyoto in AD 999—so at least they started at the top.

It's a riveting thought that Siamese warriors were reputed to train cats to sit on their shoulders and utter warning cries if the enemy approached from behind. I must start immediately training mine to do that, so that, if there is any enemy, my cats will sit on my shoulder and howl at them. Perhaps that's what Georgie Girl was doing when she used to cry all the time I sang or raised my voice!

BRITISH CATS OF THE PAST

Rumour has it that the Romans brought cats to Britain, and they came with a good reputation, having been introduced by those Phoenician traders who travelled with cats aboard for a combination of motives: practically, to keep down the rodent population which attacked their food supplies while at sea, or as a novelty to appeal to rich traders abroad, or simply because, like myself, they found cats good company. It has even been suggested that some of the cats insisted on travelling with the traders because they fancied a change of scene. Well, maybe. Anyway, by the time they were established in ancient Rome they were already popular in Italy and southern France, and for the Romans they had become a symbol of liberty. The goddess of liberty was depicted holding a cup in one hand, a broken sceptre in the other, and with a cat lying at her feet.

By the ninth century in Britain cats had successfully colonised the Isles—not to say overrun them—but, more important, they became by that time well established and highly valued. Their beginnings in most places appear to have been on a high social level

indeed—gods and goddesses among their ancestors and slaves to wait on them, to say the least, but as the centuries passed their status tended to go up and down like a yo-yo.

During their palmy early days in Britain anyone deliberately harming or killing a cat would be fined two pence, which was rather going it in those days—quite a lot of money—but the cat had to be a 'proven mouser'—a marvellous destroyer of rodents. In tenth century Wales a hamlet was legally defined as a place that contained nine buildings, one herdsman, one plow, one churn, one bull, one cock and one cat—what a strange life! With all these

From their birth until their eyes opened cats were valued at 1 penny; from then until they began to kill mice 2 pennies; and as a seasoned mouser 4 pence.

elements, the authorities were ensuring the protection of their harvest, the most important factor of country life in those times.

From their birth until their eyes opened cats were valued at 1 penny; from then until they began to kill mice 2 pennies; and as a seasoned mouser 4 pence. A penny was the

Engraved for Fox's Book of Martyrs.

A Cat hung up in Cheapside, habited like a Priest.

The sixteenth century — a bad patch for cats

value of a lamb, kid, goose or hen. If a husband and wife were separated and they owned only one cat, *he* got it. I don't think that's fair—blatant sex discrimination—but that's the way things were in those days. If an owner was convicted for killing *someone else's* cat—another example of medieval lopsided reasoning—the offender had to give its owner a sheep with her lamb or the amount of corn that would cover the cat when its corpse was suspended by its tail, with its nose touching the ground, corn being the crop that cats protected from mice and rats, of course.

It seems that after cats had had a fairly good run for their money, rot set in: by the Middle Ages cats had acquired a sinister reputation, which seems to have started with the Church, whose influence was then so strong and which should certainly have known better. The hysteria seems to have started in Europe, where people had begun to believe that the Devil was apt to appear on earth as a black cat—talk about swings and roundabouts, from one extreme to the other. Persecution reached its height in the German town of Metz, when an outbreak of St. Vitus Dance was blamed on the appearance of a black cat in 1344 and thirteen cats were publicly burned alive as the start to an epidemic of burnings, while other cats were hurled from church belfries to their death. By the end of the 15th century Pope Innocent VII instructed the Inquisition to seek out 'cat-worshippers'. So much for Infallibility: I fear that I would have had a very poor innings in those times. Women who kept cats were inevitably classified as witches and publicly burned with their pets. Atom bomb or no atom bomb, there's certainly a lot to be said for being alive in the twentieth century.

I cannot bring myself to go on about the kind of persecution to which cats, and, for that matter, people, were subjected in the reigns of Elizabeth I and James I, when the only cats or cat owners safe from torture and death were those who kept obvious mousers which had to live out in the open—never indoors—so it could not be accused of being a 'familiar' or friend of the family. Dogs seem to have escaped the witch hunt and were the only kind of pet it was safe to keep, especially for single women.

As usual, Shakespeare sums up in a single phrase the plight to which the cat's status had been reduced. In *Much Ado About Nothing* he wrote 'Hang me in a bottle like a cat'—a reference to the popular 'sport' of the time where a cat was enclosed in a bag or firkin or leather

Another view of the origin of the phrase 'letting the cat out of the bag'

bottle and hung up in a tree for archers to use as a target. This horrendous pastime seems to me to have been the origin of the saying 'letting the cat out of the bag'. I must say I laughed so much at a very very funny speech that the late Sir Ralph Richardson made when he was making an award to somebody about being told not to 'let the cat out of the bag', but I'm sure I would not have found it so funny if I'd known then what I know now.

Thank God, as mysteriously as the persecution had started it gradually petered out, and, with the swing of the pendulum, by the nineteenth century cats were not only restored to favour and prestige, but even to public office. Even by 1652 the tide was turning, when a political pamphlet was published (written by Heywood), perhaps originating the saying 'A cat may look at a king.' The meaning 'Maybe I'm below you on the social ladder but I'm as good as you are' is perhaps a fair summing up of the attitude that helped cats to survive the horrors and to thrive again to such an extent that there are now said to be between four and six million of them in the British Isles alone.

I think it must have been Charles I who inspired the above saying: the pamphlet I've mentioned was written during the first year of his reign, and Charles had a black cat which he took with him everywhere, claiming that it was his luck. When his cat died the King cried, 'My luck is gone.' How right he was: he was arrested the following day and later beheaded by order of Oliver Cromwell—the only British king to be officially executed. Some were murdered and we all know what happened to two of Henry VIII's queens, but the beheading of Charles, so movingly portrayed in the film *Cromwell* by Alec Guinness, really was one of the blackest pages in our history .

Frederick the Great, who reigned for many years during the eighteenth century—he died in 1786—made them the official guards of army food supplies and demanded of the towns he conquered that they supply him with cats for this purpose. Another long reigning monarch, Queen Victoria, owned two blue Persian cats. She left the last cat she owned, White Heather, to her son, Edward VII who ruled until 1910 and had several pet cats. He had several pet ladies, too!

Under Victoria, cats came very much into their own again, with an official status that echoed their great days in early history. New factories, new buildings, new everything were

'If mice be not reduced in number in six months, a further portion of cats' allowance must be stopped!

springing up and cats found themselves absorbed into industry, again to keep the rodents down. Under the 1868 Cat System three cats were supposed to earn 2 shillings a week between them, but the Post Office were rather mossy and only allowed 1 shilling between them, saying that they had to depend on mice to make up the rest of their wages. The Post Office, never noted for their sense of humour, issued an official statement that, 'If mice be not reduced in number in six months, a further portion of cats' allowance must be stopped!' I think they must have been sick to death of eating mice. The experiment was a success, either because the cats knew of the Secretary's threat to reduce their rations or because of a 'laudable zeal for the service'!

In 1930 the cats' wages were raised to one shilling and sixpence (about $7\frac{1}{2}$ p by present standards) and the position had come to be in many cases hereditary. A very long-lived cat called Minnie served at the Headquarters Building in London from 1938 to 1950 and was succeeded by her son Tibs, a giant cat, who weighed 231 lbs and who died in 1964—something of a celebrity, I think.

At the moment there is not much future for cats on Britain's public payroll, because job prospects are shrinking rapidly: inflation and cut-backs have taken their toll. However, to this day I subscribe to and support Cats in Industry, so obviously some are continuing to do their stuff.

CATS ARRIVE IN AMERICA

It was not until 1750 that cats were imported officially into the American colonies, again to control rodents, but there had been times, according to old English tradition, when they had more elevated, and certainly less indigestible, functions. Before the fens were drained, every household kept a cat to give warning of the floods, which the animal did by going upstairs and settling on the highest shelf, cup-board or beam. Mind you, mine do that here—they love the top of wardrobes—perhaps they know more than I guessed about the water levels of the Thames, but I take leave to doubt the whole idea. On a Sunday, according to this tradition, families took their cats to church and then for a stroll, which was known as the 'cat's walk', as a mark of their appreciation for work well done.

Names of pubs, like 'The Cat And Fiddle', again date back to the old days. This, of course, was a popular nursery rhyme: cats and kittens on the sign of the inn usually meant that large pewter measures of beer would be served. *The Cat and Fiddle* was also the title of a very jolly 'thirties musical starring Alice Delysia, the

French star, famous for her 'saucy' Ooh-la-la approach to life, but, funnily enough, it was the usually dignified Peggy Wood who sang the rather goey 'She Wouldn't Say Yes and She Wouldn't Say No' to Francis Lederer. It was a long haul from that to the Mother Superior and 'Climb Every Mountain' in *The Sound of Music*. I met Peggy Wood at a lunch at Simpsons of Piccadilly which Dorothy Dickson gave for Noel Coward and other stars who had helped her with the Stage Door Canteen. I was photographed with Noel, Dorothy and two of his other original *Bitter Sweet* stars: Peggy had done it in London, Evelyn Laye in New York and Anna Neagle did the film. I don't know why I was in the picture, because I'd had nothing to do with *Bitter Sweet*—but it was a nice souvenir to have. Peggy, Anna and Noel are, alas, no longer with us.

Almost back to where we started this brief history of the cat family—with Egypt and its quaint burial customs—in 1949 the mummified body of a cat, with the mummified body of a rat in its mouth, was found behind a wall in a house in London. It had been put there some two hundred years earlier when the house was built, to 'keep out the Devil'. And there I think we must let the matter rest.

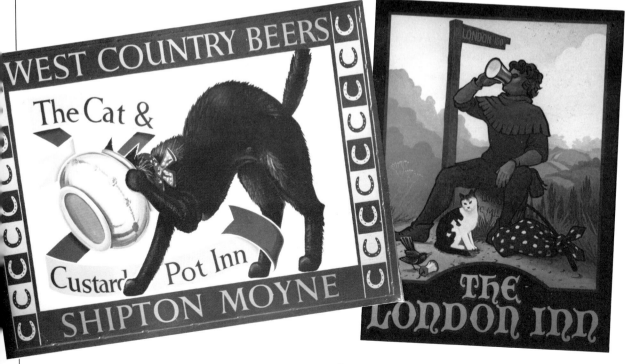

Cats Around The Honeypot

After Footy and Fred I got another lovely black kitten called Andy. As I'd got Footy I thought I'd better have hands and feet or feet and hands! He was an adorable little black cat and came from a farm, but he was slightly retarded. This was the first one of his kind I've ever come across. He simply could not judge distances and I used to watch him in the garden practising small jumps. He very unfortunately got a bad hormone condition and got fatter and fatter and I just could not comfort him during the night. I would have to turn him over or move him practically ever twenty minutes and eventually he had to be put to sleep because he was very very unhappy in his health, but, while he was alive he had a wonderful time at Honeypot. He died in 1974 after eight or nine extremely happy years with the others.

In a way theatre people are very lucky, because they have this marvellous outlet; they have to forget grief, they have to perform and they often have to be funny. In a way it's a great luxury, because if you're an ordinary person, you haven't got the outlet or the discipline of having to get on and perform and you can grieve forever, but, because we've got to get on there and do it, and it's only when we come off that we remember all the sad things.

My Lovely Footy

FURRY WEE

In 1962 I was in a summer show, *Let's Make a Night of it*, in Weston-super-Mare, the beginning of which was very unhappy because the day I left to go there my mother died at 11 o'clock in the morning. To me this was just one of the biggest tragedies of my life because she was my mentor and great supporter. Anyway, I had to leave London, where we'd been rehearsing, to go to Bristol. It's always better if you're in the midst of disaster to *have* to do something and I had to make a television appearance at Bristol with an exerpt of the show before it opened. I remember getting into the car shouting 'Mummy, Mummy' at, strangely enough, exactly the time she died. I drove to Bristol and made the television appearance. In the show, Billy Burden was our comedian and very funny doing those country sketches in a sort of smock and a straw hat in a very funny West Country sort of talk. We did several sketches together.

Then Craig Douglas came into my life and into the show—well, he had to come into the show to come into my life. He was absolutely enchanting: he had such a beautiful sort of face and he was in the record charts then. He looked—and was—extremely young and I think I referred to him as 'the Boy Virgin'. He was wonderful—I got on terribly well with him. I had a flat in Weston-super-Mare, about which my brother made a rather riveting remark. He was a scientist and rather slow thinker, and after a long stare at me he said 'D'you know, Beryl, I can see no reason at all why anyone should ever come to Weston-super-Mare for a holiday!' As the season went on I realized what he meant, because it was like breathing in hot cotton wool—you could get no air at all into your lungs.

But there were great compensations. I made friends with an old lady; I remember her name, Kay Caygill, and she's still alive, but unfortunately while I was doing a television show recently with Terry Wogan my address book was stolen so I can only remember that she lived at Bleaden, which is near Weston, and she had thirty cats. I met her again in Bristol and she was full of life and said, 'Oh, it's so awful, because my legs are so wonky!' Her husband had died but she still goes marching on, and from time to time she rings me. She was wonderful, my dresser was marvellous, and I also made friends with Elsye Monks, who played the organ, who was married at that time to Dai Francis of 'Black And White Minstrels' fame. She too was splendid and there were splendid things happening.

Two of the dancers in the show bought a tiny black kitten called Mimosa. She was a very delicate little thing that they had bought from a pet shop. These little dancers brought their kitten to the show every night in a shopping basket on the bus. I told them, 'That's really no life for her; let me look after her for the season in my flat'. She made such a noise—she seemed to have such heavy feet, or the flat was exceedingly badly built and I called her, first of all 'Fury the Wonder Horse', because there was this great thudding of hooves up and down the corridor. But, of course, that turned into 'Furry', then she became Furry Wee, because she was, and that remained her name for the rest of her life. Of course, I got so fond of her—she was a magical kitten, and at that time showed no signs of illness—that by the end of the run I said, 'Now, look here, will you let me keep her?' They by that time had completely forgotten about her and they said, 'Oh, yes, of course—you take Furry Wee back to Honeypot Cottage.' She lived happily here, but she suffered ill health. She had something like 72 cortisone injections eventually and I could no longer bear to see her go through this every day. Her health failed completely and she had to be put to sleep, because she'd never really been well. She was a very game little bird and she managed very well, but she wasn't well enough to go on living, and I can't bear to see animals suffer, so I had her put to sleep. Her lungs were like little weeny sponges—the cortisone had shrunk all her inside bits. I know this because I asked the vet if he would do a post mortem on her so that he might learn something for a future person who might have a cat in such a condition. There was really nothing of her inside left. My faith in cortisone is totally destroyed, because it is obviously a very destructive drug and people ought to be very wary before letting their cats take it.

But Furry Wee did have a very happy life here, and she was very beautiful and she knew that she was beautiful. She was only borrowed, like all our animals are, and so I had to let her go. There we are. The happy life that Furry Wee did have was four years long, so she didn't do too badly in the raffle really, although it was much too short for me.

A CAT FOR SHEILA

My advice to anybody who considers buying or obtaining a cat is not to go to a pet shop, because they are open to so much infection and disease, and are often very hard to rear. It's much better to go to the nearest RSPCA cat home where you have to sign a certificate, saying you're a fairly decent member of society and you take on the responsibility of adopting a cat. I've done this with all mine that I've had from the RSPCA—I think about eight up to now. I was replacing a cat for my friend Joan Bissett's daughter Sheila, whose cat had died. I went to a place off Baker Street when I had a flat in that area—an investment for when I was working late in the West End that eventually became far too expensive to pay off—and I had a very very nasty experience there. I bought a white Persian cat from a shop for £25. Then a woman rang me up to say she'd already bought the cat and they'd sold it twice. This poor little mite called Mandy had everything wrong with it. It had canker in its ears, it had growths on its neck—everything. I didn't know as much about cats as I do now, but these people had absolutely no right to sell it as a living, breathing cat, because it was ill and it was in a desperate condition and I spent a fortune on getting it right. The other lady who had paid the money backed out when I explained how ill the cat was—she didn't want to know about it then. This was before the days of the animal insurance Pet Plan, which I am told is absolutely marvellous both for cats and dogs, although if you have ten it just isn't practicable, and, touch wood, most of my cats of insurable age—you have to take out the policy before they are seven—are very healthy indeed. But how I could have done with it for that poor wee mite, whose sale was a fraud, from beginning to end, and I find that most animals that are purchased from pet shops, or, indeed, from markets that sell pets, are totally unreliable. Don't do it, because they don't look after them, they don't care for them, they'll palm them off on to anybody, and it isn't fair to the animal or to the future owner. If these places can't be banned altogether they should be subject to the most stringent laws and regular inspection by the RSPCA.

GEORGIE GIRL

And so to my lovely Georgie Girl. I was very surprised, in 1968, to be asked to do the film of *The Killing Of Sister George*, having done the play in London and New York. Bette Davis was strongly tipped, but in the end Robert Aldrich

A cat may look at a Queen

asked me to do it. We started on the film and were taken to the well-known Lesbian club, the Gateways in Brameson Street in London and, of course, I had never been to such a place. I must sound a bit naïve, but it's unlikely that I would have been to such a place and they took me on a Saturday night. Everybody was holding everybody's bottom and boobs and everything and I said, 'If I'd ever have seen a place like this I'd never have done the play!'

But then I'd never have met Georgie Girl. These girls gave me a wonderful birthday party in a sort of courtyard they had—you had to go downstairs to get into the club—and I never discovered why the butch ladies went into the gents' loo—no men were, of course, admitted to the club—or why lovely girls with long blonde hair went off with butch ladies, or why a lot of bent gentlemen went off with butch ladies. It was a total mystery to me. It was a riveting experience, and we, of course, were not allowed to get dressed or made up in the club and we went across the road in Chelsea to the Swan Hotel to do all that. We also had rather superior lunches there with a bottle of wine, and one day, when we were having lunch a very pretty cat came in with a white vest and paws and was otherwise quite black. I said, 'Oh, what a beautiful little cat,' because she was a *little* cat. They said, 'Oh, she's had some kittens, and we're rather looking for a home for the one that is left.' I thought, 'Here we go again. There's going to be another cat.' So I said, 'Well, I would have to ask Joan whether it's all right,' because when I go away whoever's helping me here has to be responsible—well, nobody can really be responsible for what cats do, but you know what I mean. They have to be cared for and provided for and that was something Joan was very good at. I described this tiny little kitten which was exactly like her mother, with a white front and white paws, and Joan said, 'Yes, of course have her. She sounds lovely,' and she was called Georgie Girl, mainly because I was in the film of Sister George and that I'd seen the film of *Georgie Girl* when I was in New York and I'd kept going to see it. It's rather like jokes—I love going to see the same films, like I love old jokes. I have a sort of set of a few jokes that make me laugh every time I relate them or think about them, and I don't need new things. Georgie Girl became well estab-

Fred must have heard the conversation, because the next day he was up and about, he was eating, he was drinking milk wildly—the top of the milk, mind you, which Joan gave him; I didn't get a look in. As for Georgie Girl, for the rest of his life he slept with her in his arms. If she ran up a tree he would sit at the bottom—I don't think he could have got up a tree, so he sat waiting while she did the trees. She used to skitter up the trees and he remained below waiting patiently at the bottom and he never let her out of his sight—devoted to her. They had such a wonderful sort of relationship and in fact, when Fred had a stroke Georgie Girl became a very great friend of Emma's and Emma and Georgie Girl always slept together, again in each other's arms, or like spoons.

> *He didn't stir, he didn't go to the loo, he didn't do anything; he just lay there, like a great black lump.*

lished here, but Fred went into a sort of decline in the airing cupboard. Joan and I used to go and see if he was alive: this went on for days and days. He didn't stir, he didn't go to the loo, he didn't do anything; he just lay there, like a great black lump. I said to Joan, 'I'm very worried about him—perhaps we can get the vet to give him an injection that will blot all this out of his mind, or maybe, Joan, something even worse, because I can't have him behaving like this; I dread he's going to fade out.'

EMMA AND PATRICK

Emma and her brother Patrick formed a whole new chapter in my life from 1970. When we'd finished at the Gateways, where we worked for three weeks—very happily, I might say (although some of the girls were camera-shy and were quickly spotted and removed from the film by Robert Aldrich the director who said 'Oh, they must be Civil Servants or something and they're not going to look!')—we had some locations on Hampstead Heath. I had a lot of walking to do over the titles, I remember.

Patrick Cargill,
the inspiration

Patrick

As a kitten growing
into his feet

Patrick's sister, Emma

I looked round when we got to the Heath and there was Archie, the tattooed chucker-out at the Gateways.

I said, 'Oh, Archie, I didn't expect you to be up here.' She said, 'No, well, I come, Beryl, in case any of them bent birds was after you!'

At the beginning of the run of *Blithe Spirit*, I found two little scraps of kittens at the bottom of a ditch in Coppermille Road in Wraysbury who were eating soil, because they had no food. They were tiny little things, so of course I brought them home—I mean, what else was I to do with them? One was called Patrick, after Cargill, whom I was playing with— sounds very funny, perhaps 'acting' is a better word—in Noel Coward's comedy. Patrick, like his namesake, was extremely handsome, and Emma was so called because she was like a little Jane Austen cat. She was a tabby, tiny but round, and had a sort of spotted tummy and very little stripes of tabby. She was really like the Cheshire Cat—a little Victorian thing— and she and Patrick lived in Honeypot Cottage for a very long time and very happily.

Unfortunately I noticed that Emma had a cataract and when I told the vet, he said, 'Oh, there's no such thing as cats having cataracts,' but when he came he said, 'I'm very sorry to say that you're right—she *has* got a cataract.' When I asked him if he could remove the cataract, he said 'No—well, I could, if you could make her wear big glasses.' So, unhappily, she had to have one eye removed which, at that stage of the game, meant two very big operations. She managed very well with one eye: cats are funny—their distances for getting

through places are judged by their whiskers; they are like antennae to them. They feel the space they're going through—they know whether they can get through it or not. She managed very well with one eye and was a very happy little soul.

When Patrick was quite young a Muscovy duck decided to adopt us. I called her Jemima and she was really very beautiful, white and grey with a little bright red piece on the top of her head. She arrived with three little baby

Patrick used to lie in the bushes, beckoning the baby ducks, so he could have a good meal.

ducks and Patrick used to lie in the bushes, beckoning the baby ducks, so he could have a good meal. She used to peck his bottom, which became really quite sore but I wouldn't put anything on it, because I thought if I do he's not going to learn that it's wrong. Eventually, after this great battle of the bottom Jemima and Patrick became great friends. Jemima I think was a little bit thick, really, but she was a very lovely bird to have about the place, because I used to give her cornflakes every morning on the bottom step in front of the house and she always flew around my head— that was a little salute every morning to say, 'Hello, here I am'—then eat her cornflakes and her milk, and she had all sorts of other lovely things to eat.

She arrived one morning with a gentleman duck that I called Jeremy—she'd brought him to case the joint, to see if it was suitable to lay her eggs in. She chose a very silly place to lay them, a coal bunker that I have outside. I have that smokeless fuel, which is round, and she obviously thought that the pieces of coal were black eggs, so she pulled all her down out and made a nest, which was bright black, on the coal, and laid nineteen eggs, and she sat on these eggs. Any water bird who sits on eggs has to wet her feathers twice a day, so while she was in the water wetting her feathers Patrick used to sit on the eggs, so he also was getting jet black. They were a terrible pair. She sat on the eggs for so long it became apparent Jeremy hadn't done his stuff, because they weren't fertilised at all.

In a moment of fury one day she smashed all these rotten eggs, which by then were absolutely rancid, and I thought that was the end of it. But not at all. She was missing for a couple of days and I was at Eileen Craigton's house—Lord and Lady Craigton live up the river, where the river is very wide—and I said, 'That's Jemima over there!' I called her and she came swimming across the river. Eileen said, 'It's a seagull' and I said 'No, it's not, it's Jemima.' She couldn't get up, because they haven't got steps up to their garden, only a rather big step down, so I said, 'Go home, Jemima' and she swam down to Honeypot Cottage. She was very bright with me—only a little thick when it came to her eggs. She laid another nineteen eggs under the steps leading from the French doors I've got and the same performance went on again. She didn't bring Jeremy this time—I think she was a bit cheesed off with him. She sat on the eggs again and Patrick did the same thing—sat on them when she went in the water; she was a bit cleaner this time as she wasn't sitting on coal. She still had her cornflakes every morning and flew round my head and seemed very happy, but, again, the eggs were no go, so eventually she smashed those: they get in a terrible state when they know there's no life in them.

One day I said to Joan, 'Oh, Jemima does look a poor poor thing.' She'd flown round my head but she looked very poor in health and feathers and everything. I don't know what had happened to her—they're very difficult to rear, Muscovy ducks, I've since grown to realize. The next day Joan found her floating in the river, dead. She'd been with us for four years—just found and adopted us—and she was very happy while she was here and Patrick's great mate. How Patrick managed not to break the eggs he sat on so devotedly is one of life's little mysteries. He was, I must say, a most lovable and very handsome cat and while he lived here he was the King of the Castle. He was the first one in the pecking order, as it were, except for the little period that Jemima got at him. I don't think I've ever seen such a beautiful cat; it looked as if he had make-up on—the sort of make-up that a ballet dancer puts on, with a lot of black lines round his eyes to make them look enormous.

Later in his life I looked at him and I

thought, 'Oh dear, he's really not at all well.' There were no visible signs, his coat was O.K. but it was his face: his face wasn't right, and only I could know that.

I telephoned Brian Woodward, my vet, and told him I didn't think Patrick was at all well. He came to have a look at him and said, 'I'd like to have him in for a few days'—which, of course, is something I absolutely dread. I'm such a fool about the cats going to the vet's and I behave so badly if I have to go with them. I said, 'Well, all right—that's fine, take him with you.' They did a brain scan, which I didn't know that you could do for cats, at his surgery at Hampton Court. Patrick had a slight tumour on his brain and Brian said, 'There is something wrong inside and I'd like to do an exploratory operation. Would you be in agreement with that?' I said, 'Yes, of course—anything to really make him better.'

He rang me in the middle of the operation and told me that he had a growth going right through the middle of his liver. He could patch him up and let him come home, if I wanted but I said, 'No, I wouldn't like you to. I love him too much. Just tell him I love him and give him some more anaesthetic and let him go to sleep and he won't ever know about it.'

It's terribly sad if you have to have animals put to sleep and hold them in your arms while they do it, but that was about the saddest thing because I wasn't with him. This was what upset me so much. All the others I'd been with. Patrick was just in somebody else's house and somebody else's hands and I could do nothing to help him. He had such a wonderful life, which I must remember, he'd been so happy and we'd had such marvellous games.

He was very funny, because, when he was absolutely swinging, the extraordinary things he liked to eat were cabbage stalks and roses—if anybody sent me roses I had no chance, because Patrick used to pick them out of the vase and eat them. There was something about roses that drove him mad. So, it was a sad ending, but he really did have a beautiful life.

At the time that Patrick had to die I was in a revue, a frightfully jolly show called *A Little Bit On The Side* and I wasn't going to tell anybody. It was directed by Billy Chappell who is a very dear friend of mine and who also paints cats—he does the most wonderful, extraordinary portraits of cats—and I looked at his face and I just had to tell him, and have a bit of a cry.

I remember saying to Eric Braun, who brought Dorothy Dickson to see the show at Richmond, 'Do tell Dorothy if I'm a bit off or if I'm a bit unfunny tonight in the dressing-room it's just because my darling Patrick has gone and it's something that is very hard to recover from.' So, of course, everybody understood.

KATH

People who love animals do understand that their little lives are, as I've said before, only borrowed, but while we have them with us they give such joy and companionship that the shortness of the time they're with us is a price we pay, not gladly, but with understanding and thankfulness for their lives. Joe Orton in his short and tragic life had a great deal to say about life and death—seen through his own very individual and mocking, not to say savage humour.

Never was this more in evidence than in *Entertaining Mr. Sloane* and I was delighted to be asked to do the film although the location did turn out to be Camberwell Cemetery. It's a very eerie cemetery, with a larger than lifesize—about 7 ft. 6 in. statue of Freddie Mills, with his boxing gloves crossed at his feet, among a lot of very extraordinary tombstones. It was a very funny film but, like all Joe Orton's work, slightly on the eerie side.

There was a tiny little kitten running about there and I took a great shine to her and

I thought, 'Surely I'm not dead yet.'

she to me. One day I saw a little gaggle of gravediggers arriving at the lodge house by the gates where the film unit was set up. I thought, 'Surely I'm not dead yet' but, no, they'd come as a deputation, almost touching their forelocks. They all took their caps off and their spokesman said, 'We believe, Miss, that you've become very fond of our cat'—she was *tiny*—they pushed him to the front and he said, 'We'd like to make you a formal presentation of her!'

'How lovely,' I said, 'I'd *love* to take her home,' so, of course, she was called Kath, after

the character I was playing in the film. It was amazing—Camberwell Cemetery is on a huge main road, with these long distance heavy lorries rumbling past all the time—you can imagine the trouble we had with the sound equipment and the dubbing sessions that went on afterwards—that's adding your voice to the picture. Kath had crossed that road as a tiny baby hundreds of times and then she came to Honeypot Cottage, which is in the country, away from all the noise and danger, and survived only two years.

She was an enchanting tabby with a white front, but a very demanding little madam. Her great thing was sitting on top of the television that's at the side of my bed and lolling over so far to look at the picture that she knocked the set over several times and I had to keep ringing the firm up that I rent the television from to say, 'I'm afraid my television's broken again!' Of course, I couldn't tell them that she'd crashed it to the floor.

One day she was missing and I couldn't understand it. I called and I called and I called her. I went to everybody's house, I looked in everybody's garage and I couldn't find her. And then I went to the boatyard which is down a lane near the cottage. I said to somebody at the boatyard, where father and son were building a boat, 'When you came to the boatyard this morning'—which must have been pretty early—'did you see a tabbycat with a white front?'

The old gentleman said, 'I have to ask my son.' The son came out of what was nearly a boat and said, 'No, we haven't seen anything—

nothing—we haven't seen anything.' They'd both got very red faces, so I knew that they'd knocked her over or hit her or something with the car when they were belting to the boatyard.

The people next door to me at that time, Mr. and Mrs. Jackson, took their dog for a walk that night and the dog found Kath, who was, unfortunately then, a stiff. I went with a basket and brought her home. It was only a hundred yards from where I live. Since then I've always called that part of the road Kath's Leap, because she was obviously coming across the field, having done a bit of naughty hunting, to come home for her breakfast, and they caught her on the way back.

She was an excessively happy cat, cherished and enjoyed during her brief stay at Honeypot. She had a short life but a gay one.

Fame And The Feline

So many famous people in the past and the present love and enjoy having cats, and the cats themselves have evidently loved and appreciated those owners who cared for them properly. Poets, philosophers, writers of all kinds, people in the entertainment world, and what I call the 'civilians', those millions who support us by coming to see us work and without whose support we'd be poor indeed, in every way—all have enjoyed the company of cats through the ages, and I'd like to make a selection of some of the most rewarding. Some are born felines—others have fame thrust upon them when they are created by the world's great writers.

I once made a record of Lewis Carroll's *Alice in Wonderland* with a lot of famous people playing the characters and the then small Karen Dotrice as Alice. I was the Duchess—a rather rough character, really—and Dirk Bogarde was the Narrator, presumably chosen personally by the Cheshire Cat because he knew Dirk to be a well-known cat lover. The Cat keeps appearing and then disappearing, bit by bit. Sir John Tenniel's original illustrations show him to have looked very much like my Emma, and Alice found him a tiny bit of a puzzlement. As she says, 'I have often seen a cat without a grin—but a grin without a

cat . . .' Well, I think I know exactly how she felt.

Jeremy Bentham, the English philospher who was born in 1748 and lived until 1832, had a cat whom he fed macaroni at his table. He 'knighted' the cat Sir John Langbourne. As Sir John grew older, he became very much more sedate, which they are, of course, inclined to do, and Bentham retitled him the Reverend John Langbourne, and when he was truly venerable, the Reverend Doctor John Langbourne.

From the sublime to the magnificently eccentric—'Divine' was the term applied to her by her admirers—Sarah Bernhardt loved the big cats, not the little ones, because she did nothing by halves, and their chances of survival would, in any case, have been exceedingly slim. She used to have the most riveting afternoons and soirées surrounded by people. I don't know where she found the energy to do it, but who ever attended her gatherings had to be brave enough to have leopards and lions and tigers leaping about the place. Maybe this explains her wooden leg—perhaps one of the lions got it. Another of her little quirks, when she travelled on the trains on Sundays (presumably to the equivalent of the Monday morning band-call) was to carry with her a great chest full of money because she thought it was very good to have 'ready money'. I must say I agree. I seldom have it, but its very nice if you have got a few of the 'readies'. I hope she made more generous use of her readies than one of her contemporaries, almost, Nellie Wallace (you might say 'sublime to ridiculous' in her case, but only because she ridiculed herself, with her funny little hat with a feather and her elastic sided boots when she sang 'My Mother Said Always Look Under the Bed—to See if There's a Man About'). When I was very very young and starting out in the business I appeared in shows with her and was riveted by the fact that when she got the porter to carry her cabin trunk from the station at Bedford to the stage door she paid him threepence; Nellie probably wasn't a cat lover, because she travelled with a parrot.

Chaucer, several centuries before either of these great ladies of the theatre, one of England's earliest and greatest poets and the first to be at all widely read, because he lived in the very first days of printing, understood better than most people that if you wanted a cat to catch and kill mice you had to feed him properly to build up his energy, which of course makes very good sense. He writes about cats having plenty of milk and meat ('fostre him well with milk and tendre flessh'), not just any old scraggy bits. You should provide him with somewhere comfortable to sleep, 'and make his couche of silk.' You play your part and he'll play his, which sounds like perfectly good sense to me.

Matthew Arnold, the great poet of some four hundred years later, wrote an elegy to his canary, *Poor Mathias* and saw cats as something much more sinister and significant than a domestic pet. Presumably he was smarting over poor Mathias' end when he wrote:

'Cruel, but composed and bland,
  Dumb, inscrutable and grand,
So Tiberius might have sat,
  Had Tiberius been a cat'!

Well, he certainly wasn't one of the great cat lovers of history, but he did have a way with words—you can get the picture perfectly.

A very different sort of writer of more recent times and even more notable in his own way in the halls of fame, saw what he called 'Felix Domesticus' through very different eyes. Winston Churchill had a black cat called Nelson, whom he took to Downing Street when he became Prime Minister. A chair was kept for Nelson in the Cabinet Room next to the Prime Minister and a place was reserved for him at the dining table. He often had Nelson on his bed while he was working in the morning. I've got actually three on *my* bed this morning. One day in 1943, while he was getting better from influenza, he was visited by one of his Ministers while Nelson was lying on his feet on the bed.

His Majesty's Minder

*What perfect taste – drawings of
Winston Churchill's cat*

Winston Churchill said, 'That cat is doing more for the war effort than you are. He acts as a hot-water bottle, and saves fuel, power and energy!'

One day a black kitten turned up on the doorstep of 10, Downing Street and was taken in on the 10th October, 1953, the day of Churchill's speech to the Conservative Party at Margate. That evening, as Winston was really savouring the success of his speech and the most important demonstration of his recovery from a second stroke, the kitten jumped up on to his knee. He said, 'He's brought me luck—he shall be called Margate.'

He was presented with another cat on his 88th birthday by his friend Sir John (Jock, as he was called) Colville. The cat, whom he naturally called Jock, lived at Chartwell and became popular with visitors when the house was opened to the public. When Jock died in January 1975, the curators of Chartwell had to replace him with another cat called Jock to keep the public happy! You can easily be fooled by cats, you know. The new Jock was provided for in Sir Winston's will, which stipulated that a marmalade cat should be in 'Comfortable Residence' at Chartwell for ever. He left a sum to money to cover the cat's board and lodgings.

The Savoy Hotel is very proud to have a large statue of a black cat in memory of Sir Winston Churchill in the Pinafore Room, where he used to spend a lot of time. If a party of 13 wishes to be seated in that room, the cat's statue is placed in the 14th chair to avoid any bad luck.

Churchill, I must say, was one of my great

Cat statue at the Savoy

heroes. My poor mother did suffer during the war, because, you see, every morning before my father went to his office—he was an estate agent, valuer and auctioneer—she used to convince him that we were going to win the war because of the Prime Minister, but by lunch time he'd meet a man who said we weren't, so she had to do it all over again. She had a very tough time but, like me, thought that he was a remarkable man.

In 1812 another great gift had come our way, in the form of Charles Dickens. He cherished a cat called William, whom he had to re-name Wilhelmina when 'he' presented the author with a litter of kittens. Dickens kept one cat out of the litter and called him the Master's Cat. He was quite right to do so, because this cat had the habit of using his paw to snuff out the candle in the evening to get Charles Dickens' attention. I think it was rather a hint that he ought to go to bed.

waiting in her chair when I entered, her paws folded on the tablecloth, her smooth forehead held up to be kissed like a well-bred little girl who is politely affectionate to relations and other people.' If she was inclined to refuse her soup he had only to say, 'Mademoiselle, a young lady who is not hungry for soup is not

This cat had the habit of using his paw to snuff out the candle in the evening to get Charles Dickens' attention.

Dickens' great contemporary across the channel, Alexandre Dumas, the novelist and dramatist had a cat called Mysouff I, who lived with Dumas and his mother. He said the cat ought to have been a dog, because it would meet him at the corner of the street when he came home in the evening and accompany him there in the morning—an experience I have frequently shared, only in my case there are often ten of them! Mysouff I was succeeded by Mysouff II.

Also living at this time (1811—72), which seems to have been a particularly good period for cats with an artistic turn of mind, was the poet Théophile Gautier who had a well-mannered black cat called Eponine after a character in Victor Hugo's, *Les Misérables*. If he was dining alone a place was set for her at the table, recalling Winston Churchill's four-legged friend, Nelson, and I find his description of her behaviour quite riveting: She was always

expected to have an appetite for fish' to make her lap it up! Quite a unique couple, I'd say, and I rather love Gautier's observation about cats: 'A cat can be your friend, but never your slave.'

Somehow Eponine's demure behaviour at table took my mind back to one of my favourite childhood stories, Beatrix Potter's lovable Mrs. Tabitha Twitchet and her family: Tom Kitten, who could not help tearing his trousers all the time, and his sisters Moppet and Mittens.

That most rugged and far-from-whimsical character and writer Ernest Hemingway had thirty cats in his lovely hillside home in Havana. 'A cat', he says, 'has absolute emotional honesty.' That is true. When he and his wife lived in Paris, they left their baby son, whenever they went out, in the care of a sensible yellow-eyed cat called F. Puss, who sat up erect, like a nanny, keeping guard. So who says Sir James Barrie was silly to invent a big dog called Nana as nursemaid for Mr. and Mrs. Darling's children in *Peter Pan*? Mind you, I hope F. Puss was more effective than Nana, who, after all, did let Peter Pan spirit the children away to the Never-Never Land! Hemingway's favourite cats, who surely must have included F. Puss, liked mangoes and avocados—not bad taste, because those are two of my favourite things.

Dr. Samuel Johnson was another whose cats tended to have an exotic taste in food: He was devoted to his cat Hodge to such an extent that he used to go out himself and buy oysters for him, thinking that the servants might resent having to do this and take their revenge on poor old Hodge. So it seems that one of the most dogmatic (no pun intended here) characters in literary history did have his soft spots, after all. It makes him much more endearing: I wonder if Boswell was given such favours, or did Hodge corner the market in the Johnson oysters?

Edward Lear, artist and writer during those very productive years from late Georgian times, through the Regency to Queen Victoria, was passionately devoted to his cat Foss, to such an extent that he built himself an exact replica of his former house so that Foss would not be upset when they moved. No doubt Foss was the inspiration for *The Owl And The Pussycat*, the poem about the beautiful pussycat who went sailing with an amorous owl to dance by the light of the moon before they got married, using the ring at the end of a friendly pig's nose to plight their troth!

Going back quite a bit, to Sir Isaac Newton, who is not to be trifled with—the great

Edward Lear's cat – typical!

philosopher was born in 1642 and lived to 85—had two cats, and so he made two holes in his door, one for his big cat and a smaller one for her kittens, maybe adapting his theory of what goes up must come down to what goes out must come back—so he was really the originator of the cat flap, you might say.

A few princes of the Church—a couple of Popes and a Cardinal or two, no less, have been noted cat supporters—Cardinal Richelieu being a staunch ally at a time when they most needed it, during the terrible persecutions of the sixteenth to seventeenth century. I have a special feeling for the Cardinal, so remarkably brought to life by George Arliss in the film of the 'thirties because I used to do an impersonation of him when I was starting out as an impressionist! 'Let them barricade the doors, let them barricade the windows: when the army comes they will batter down the walls— and the echo of those blows will awake all Paris!' How's that, from off the top of my head? The real Cardinal Richelieu had a room in the Palace which he used as a cattery, where two attendants waited on the animals, feeding them morning and evening on pâté made from chicken breasts. They should be so lucky. He left a considerable sum of money to the 14 cats who survived him, whose names included Pyramus, Thisbe and Lucifer.

It seems that there was one law for the rich and another for the poor in those days even in the cat world. The popes themselves had their little ways when it came to cats: Leo XII who lived from 1760 to 1829 personally raised the cat Micetto, a large greyish-red cat with black stripes who was born in the Vatican. He used to feed him with his own hands, like Pius IX, a throw-back to Gautier's Eponime, whose puss used to arrive with the soup and sit 'silent and respectful' facing the Pope until he had finished his meal. Thereupon he too was given his food from the hands of the Pope. It may well have been this Pope whose cat used to sit on his knee, hidden in the folds of his robes, while he gave audiences. Cardinal Wolsey's cat used to attend mass when the Cardinal was celebrating.

Back in 570–632 AD lived Mahomed, founder of the Moslem religion and author of the Koran. His beloved cat was called Meuzza, and used to sleep on his robe. One day while Meuzza was sleeping on the robe, the Prophet was summoned to his prayers: rather than disturb the cat he cut off the sleeve. When the cat woke up he arched his back in appreciation and Mahomed stroked him three times, assuring Meuzza a permanent place in the Islamic Paradise and granting all cats perpetual freedom from the danger of falling by granting them the ability always to land on their feet. A charming thought, especially because it ensured the cat an honoured place among the countless followers of Mahomed. The Christian religion did no such service, and during the Middle Ages declared that animals were incapable of having souls and therefore would be ill-treated as the 'faithful' felt inclined. At one point it even questioned whether animals had any real feelings, giving the nod for some of the appalling cruelty that persists to this day.

W. B. Yeats, the Irish poet, who died in 1939, once went to collect his fur coat at the Abbey Theatre, Dublin and found a cat lying asleep on it. He promptly followed the example of Mahomed by cutting a piece out of the coat rather than disturbing the sleeper. Other extremes in history concerning attitudes to cats are, on the one hand, Florence Nightingale, who at one time owned 60 cats (perhaps a little extreme) and never in later life travelled without one, and on the other hand, Napoleon and Caesar who disliked them intensely. Presumably Caesar made an exception for the kitten belonging to Cleopatra as portrayed by

Vivien Leigh in the film *Caesar and Cleopatra*, at the time when they were going 'steady'. Or maybe his dislike for her kitten is the reason why she turned to Mark Anthony. Will we ever know?

I mention in passing that Christopher Milne, the original Christopher Robin of *Win-*

Christopher Milne asked for a pregnant cat as his luxury on Desert Island Discs.

nie the Pooh fame, and son of one of my favourite writers, A. A. Milne, asked for a pregnant cat as his luxury on Desert Island Discs—strange thought, but he was obviously keen on founding his own Dynasty, although, of course you're not really allowed to take a living thing into the island. Their namesake, Betty Milne, my dresser in the theatre (whom I always call my Minder, because she does look after me so well) had a beautiful cat called Toddles, who used to go everywhere with her and her family in the car. He travelled quite free, not in a basket. My cats couldn't bear to travel like that, but Toddles was his own cat and did his own thing. On one occasion he was taken to Scotland and just jumped in the car like a dog does, before they set off. When they arrived they left Toddles to play round the car, as they always did, with his food ready for him inside. It is remarkable that they could do that. Mine would just run, because to them going in the car means going to the vet, but I suppose if you start very

early, taking them for little car rides, they would get used to it.

Betty, her husband Bob and her son Gordon, who was then quite small, came back to the car and—no Toddles. They looked and they looked for hours, with Gordon crying and everybody in a terrible state, and in the end could wait no longer, because they had to get back to London. In despair Betty said, 'Well, we'll just have to go, and notify the hotel that he's lost.' She got into the back of the car and looked down and there were two lovely great big eyes looking up into hers. Of course, it was Toddles. He was sitting under the front seat— he'd got fed up with Scotland and walking round, and there he was, waiting to go home. All their hours of searching had been in vain.

Betty is in very good company with others who, through the years have had or known unique felines. Of course, every cat *is* unique, especially to every owner, like every dog and

Every cat is unique, especially to every owner, but some are more unique than others.

every child to its parents, but some are more unique than others and some have even made their mark in history.

President Coolidge of the USA had a canary called Caruso, who could imitate the voice of the great opera singer. Caruso developed a great fondness for a cat called Timmie, to whom he used to sing while the cat sat enthralled. Eventually the President had to make a present of Caruso to Timmie and the bird would walk up and down his back and sit between his front paws. Obviously, love conquers all, and some cats have strange preferences, like the poet Dante's cat, who liked nothing better than to sit holding a lighted candle between his forepaws. Perhaps the sight of this risky pleasure inspired Dante's Inferno, but who knows? Anyway, the bitter-sweet ending to the romance between Timmie and Caruso was that the bird died one day while singing to the cat. They really qualified to be included amongst the great lovers of history, and may well have inspired the title of that most funny but chilly movie *The Cat And The Canary*, starring Bob Hope and Paulette Goddard.

On the same theme, but down to earth with a bump, is the story of a life-saving cat. An elderly lady used to seek protection, in World War II, with her cat and dog and canary under her oak dining table, whenever she hadn't time to reach the air-raid shelter, because often they weren't in very convenient places. One day she was standing in the porch when the cat suddenly leapt indoors and dashed under the table. She, very sensibly, followed with her dog and canary. A few minutes later a bomb exploded in the garden, demolishing the porch and blowing in the windows. Had it not have been for the cat they would all have been killed.

At St. Paul's Cathedral there was a resident cat called Faith, a stray rescued from a burning building during the Blitz when she refused to leave her kitten. When she died in 1948, after twelve happy years at St. Paul's, a plaque to her memory was donated by the PDSA to 'The Bravest Cat in the World' to celebrate this heroic deed. The PDSA is another charity devoted to the care of sick animals and I have always been happy to do work for such a wonderful cause. At Faith's funeral service, held in Holy Trinity Church, local children had an open invitation to bring their pets. The service was attended by dozens of cats, kittens, ducks, chickens, a Pekinese, a bull mastiff, a lamb, and—would you believe?—a minnow in a jar. This must have been pleasing to the Management—which is how I think of God—because when He made the world He gave each animal whatever gift it desired and the cat went to the end of the line, very unlike today's cats. To the elephant and bear He gave strength; the rabbit and deer swiftness; the owl the ability to see at night; birds and butterflies beauty; the fox cunning; the monkey intelligence; the dog loyalty; the lion courage; the otter playfulness. To the cat at the end of the line He said, 'What will you have?' The cat replied, 'Oh, whatever scraps you have over.' God said, 'But I am the Management—I have everything left over.' And the cat said, 'Then I'll have a little of everything, please.' So God gave him everything, but took away his false modesty and also gave him a gentle purr.

That day the cat was really honoured by her peers for all her qualities, including the courage of the lion and the loyalty of the dog.

Noble guardsman—the cat from the BM

CAT CELEBRITIES

Here we have to pay tribute again to some working cats who, in their time, reached celebrity status. Mike was a cat who reigned supreme at the British Museum—in fact, he welcomed visitors there for 19 years. Then, at Whitehall, there were a succession of working cats, all black and all called Peter, since 1833. The last cat of that name held his job for 16 years from 1948 to 1964. Round his neck he wore this little identity tag—'Peter, Home Office, SW1'. He killed hundreds of rats for his keep and earned 2/6 a week from the Treasury—another evidence of inflation on the march. In 1958, R. A. Butler, the then Home Secretary, put Peter's picture on his Christmas cards and Peter enjoyed a brief moment of fame, which, from time to time, we all hope we

do. When he died, which was unfortunately of liver trouble, which cats do get, two Home Office Librarians and a Shetland pony called Goldie were graveside mourners. Government workers chipped in with £8 to buy him an oak-veneered coffin with brass handles. Peter is buried in the PDSA's cemetery at Ilford, next to the grave of Coco, a mouse. Peter was succeeded by a tribute to Women's Lib called Peta, who retired in 1974.

There are several records of Champion Mousers: the champion British rodent destroyers were the corporation cats. A female tabby killed 12,480 rats for the White City Stadium in London during a six-year period— I wonder who kept count?—and a male tabby cat called Mickey eliminated about 1,000 mice a year from the premises of Shepherd and Sons in Lancashire through the 23 years he worked

✳ 10 out of 10 for mousing

for them. He died, sadly, in 1968. I am horrified by this sort of information, because I know how extremely bad it is for cats to eat mice. It makes them have those round worms in their lungs and also defaces their skins with little scabs and things. It really isn't a healthy thing to be a mouser.

And now we come to Fat Albert. He was a tomcat who was the official blood donor for cats at the Marlton Animal Hospital in New Jersey in the early 1970's. Fat Albert, who arrived as a beat-up stray did so well and became so huge and healthy after hospital staff took him in and cared for him that he gave blood regularly to cats in need of a transfusion. He died in 1982 after having done a great deal of good work in his life.

Up the social ladder again—Wilberforce, white and black splotches and a black tail, was requisitioned from the RSPCA at Hounslow in 1973 to deal with vermin at Downing Street—

> *He did enjoy special perks :*
> *the police were instructed*
> *to ring the frontdoor bell*
> *at any time to let him in.*

oh, dear, there we go again—when Edward Heath was Prime Minister. However, he did enjoy special perks: the police were instructed to ring the frontdoor bell at any time to let him in. Now 13, he has served under four Prime

Wilberforce seeks an audience with Mrs T

Ministers—Heath, Wilson, Callaghan and Thatcher—and has always been popular among his colleagues, receiving his share of fan mail and Christmas cards. I wonder if Mrs. T has a tiny Honour for him up her sleeve: he

Railway cat Tiddles is dead

IT IS the end of the line for the mighty moggie, master of the ladies loo at Paddington Station. Tiddles is dead.

The 32lb tom padded his way into a domain where all men fear to tread, and he reigned supreme for 13 years.

The cat, who hated the noise of the high-speed trains, wandered into the loo when he was six weeks old and was instantly adopted by Miss June Watson.

He made it quite clear from the beginning that his diet was not that of a common street cat. Tiddles had his own fridge, containing liver, rabbit, chicken and steak.

He became part of the station's history and won more acclaim than the station's mascot, Paddington Bear.

Passengers often made special journeys to visit Tiddles, who also became an international star when Canadian and New Zealand film crews featured him.

Fan mail which poured in from all over the world was answered by Miss Watson.

Earlier this year Tiddles walked off with the prize for the biggest feline in London in Capital Radio's Big Cat Competition.

His basket resembled a throne and was decorated for special occasions such as Prince Charles' wedding and Tiddles 13th birthday last month.

Miss Watson, who has worked for British Rail for 42 years, turned down redundancy two years ago because she could not bear to part Tiddles from what he called home.

Master of the ladies' loo, Paddington

certainly seems to be a deserving case!

Another very famous cat was Tiddles who lived at Paddington Station for fourteen years in the Ladies' Loo. Actually, I've never been there, so I never had the pleasure of meeting him. He was fed devotedly by the constant stream of passers-by and got very fat—$2\frac{1}{2}$ stone, no less—the second largest cat in Britain. He was a huge silver-grey tabby with big bulbous eyes. The Area Manager confessed that he never actually saw him, presumably because he never went into the Ladies Loo. I wonder if Tiddles could appear and disappear at will, like the Cheshire Cat? Poor old Tiddles died in 1983, in his natural environment. R.I.P.

Sugar was a cream-coloured part Persian—I know exactly what everybody means by that, because they're a race apart—with a deformed left hip, and he was so frightened of riding in a car that his owners, Mr. and Mrs. Woods gave him to a neighbour in California in 1951 when they moved to Oklahoma. Fourteen months later Sugar arrived in the Woods' barn, having walked the 1,500 miles—a horrifying and quite mind-defying thought. It really was a case of *Lassie Come Home*, which we're inclined to think of as a romantic tale for children. In this case substitute *Sugar Come Home* and I hope to the greatest welcome any animal ever had.

It may be an old wives' tale—there are so many old wives, and so many tales—but when my cats are going to be let out of the spare room where they've been brought up, I always put butter on their paws and they make a great performance of licking the butter off. This does seem to stop them from straying. I have been asked if margarine would do, and I have to say I don't think in this case margarine would be a decent substitute: it's got to be best butter or nothing!

I think that if Sugar's marathon trek is not in the *Guinness Book of Records* it jolly well should

Underneath that fat there is a cat

be, along with such items as the heaviest recorded cat in Britain (an 11-year old male tabby called Poppa in Newport, who weighed $44\frac{1}{2}$ lbs in November 1984) and the oldest recorded cat, a tabby called Puss, who celebrated its 36th birthday on 28 November 1939 and died the next day. It really was a case of *Back to Methuselah*.

I would like to end this round-up of Fame and the Feline in almost all of its aspects on a light social note and a back-to-the-theatre glance. Tiger the 'Terror of the Ritz Hotel' was a colossal mouser fed on every luxury. (So why

Tiger had to be sent away annually on a slimming course.

did he want to eat mice? When Will They Ever Learn, When Will They Ever Learn?, I can hear Dietrich chanting through the ages.) Tiger had to be sent away annually on a slimming course. The Stafford Hotel still has a bar cat called Whisky. The head barman, Charles Guano, bought a cat for the bar called Jubilee, but someone stole her and he replaced her with two black and white females from the same litter called Whisky and Soda about nine years ago. Soda died in 1985 but Whisky is still there, referred to by Charles as 'he' because she's been spayed. That's the easiest way of having a sex change that I've ever heard about. Whisky is a great favourite with customers: 'he' used to bring mice back from St. James's Park and play with them in the bar, which is supposed to have pleased lady customers no end. What a funny

lot they must be. Anyway Charles promises to get Whisky, who has many hidden talents, to autograph copies of this book for the customers: he (Charles) has been head barman for 27 years and is Whisky's Minder. He says the cat is looked after better than any guest. Well, that's something, I suppose!

In my years in pantomime I only played *Dick Whittington* once. I should say 'in' *Dick Whittington*, because he was played by the golden-haired singer of ballads that used to get into the charts—Gary Miller. He, like Tommy Cooper, who was also in the pantomime, is sadly no longer with us. As in *Puss in Boots*, a cat figures largely in the panto, which has one of the most complicated plots imaginable, but is based on a lovely legend about the poor youth, wrongly accused of theft, who sets out with his cat to walk to Nottingham to seek his fortune. Happily, for both of them, they get no further than Highgate Hill, when Dick hears the bells chiming 'Turn Again, Whittington, Lord Mayor of London.' In next to no time they and the whole cast are whisked off aboard ship to Morocco, where the Sultan often turns out to have a strong voice and be either Edmund Hockridge or John Hanson.

In fact, Dick Whittington was three times Lord Mayor of London, between 1358 and 1423. His Cat is portrayed in two sixteenth century portraits, there is also a portrait in Westminster Abbey and a stone effigy on the top of Highgate Hill, where Dick did his Turn, after hearing the chimes. I understood that when a boat was commissioned to sail abroad, in this case to Morocco, people used to send whatever they possessed as a gift and it was called a Venture. The legend has it, and no one knows whether this is true, that Dick sent his Cat because that was all he possessed at the time. The Sultan of Morocco was so delighted with this gift because his land was absolutely infested by rats (and Whittington's cat was supposed to be the best ratter of his time) and the cat did the ruler a great favour by killing off all the vermin. Dick and his Trusty Pussy were rewarded with jewels and money galore, so he became rich enough to become Lord Mayor of London. Of course, whether that is true, is something that you and I have to decide. It would be lovely if it were and I am indebted to author Faith Hines of Tunbridge Wells, who sent me a fascinating little book on the subject.

It appears that Richard Whittington, or Whytyngtone or Whytyngdon, was the third son of Sir William Whittington of Pauntley in Gloucestershire. The likely year of his birth was 1359. Later when he had made his fortune he was a mercer, among his customers was the Earl of Derby, who became King Henry IV. He and his son Henry V were perpetually embarrassed by lack of the 'readies' and Whittington was one of their chief bankers. He died in 1473, the last year of his term of office.

Faith Hines has also shed light on one or two puzzling sayings, including a 'Cat nap', which means a sham sleep, like that of a hunting cat watching a mouse or rat. 'Cat's Paw' means to be the tool of another, from the fable of the Naughty Monkey, who wanted to get some hot chestnuts from the fire. The crafty ape took the paw of the cat to retrieve them from the hot ashes. A 'Cat Call' which some of us have experienced in the theatre at one time or another, was once an ivory whistle, used by the theatre audience to express impatience .

The term Cheshire Cat comes from the cheese, formerly sold in Cheshire, moulded like a cat. The expression 'Grins like a Cheshire Cat' is nowadays applied to people who show not only their teeth but their gums when they laugh. So now we know, and thanks very much for the information.

I remember, too some of those charming childhood cat poems of which Faith has reminded me, like:

> 'Pussy-cat, Pussy-cat, where have you been?
> I've been to London to look at the Queen.'

Well, so have I, and I can only hope that the cat in the poem had half as lovely a day as I did.

Attitudes To Cats At Home And Abroad

Cats, according to law, have never really done terribly well. As you know, until recently you were compelled to have a dog licence. It's a common belief that cats are beyond the law and that no cat owner can be responsible for the actions of his or her pet. I totally agree with that, because it's practically impossible to prevent a cat from trespassing. All you can do is hope that wherever it does go it will be welcome and if it's not welcome will be able to get out quick enough, to protect itself in this way. I've been very lucky, because my nearest neighbours for years have thought it was wonderful when my cats went to sit on their lawn and look at the river with them, but I suppose not everybody else is so lucky.

In fact, I know they're not. One night when I came home, written on a fence which is adjacent to my house was 'Death to all cats!', which made a nasty cold shiver go up my spine. Chris and I did wash it off as soon as we could. Obviously some children had done it—they can be pretty tough with cats.

If a motorist knocks over a cat he or she is not obliged to report the matter to the police or to anyone, but if a dog is run over it has to be reported. Where cats are concerned the matter rests on the conscience of the driver, and

I'm afraid some of them are totally without conscience: anyone who can knock over a child or a grown-up and speed on without even stopping to see what harm has been done, or even if the victim is still alive, is unlikely to stop for a dog, still less a cat. Sometimes it's a case of sheer panic, or even, can you imagine, concern over the loss of a no-claims bonus—whatever the reason, the attitude is quite inexcusable.

We have seen how in ancient times the cat was protected by law in the British Isles; the one about 'seasoned mousers' and the penalties to which anyone killing a neighbour's cat were liable, dates back to AD 936 in Wales. In old Saxony about the same time Henry the Fowler—whoever he was—dictated that a fine of 60 bushels of corn had to be paid by anybody killing a cat which could still catch mice; corn, of course, being the crop which cats protected from rodents. Cars at that time were hardly even a dim vision of the future, but presumably if a cat was knocked down by a cart or chariot it came under the general law of protection of those times.

Attitudes to cats have, of course, varied quite dramatically, as our brief look at their history has shown, from age to age and from country to country. We saw how very lucky

Japanese homage to a dead cat ⟶

they were considered to be in China; they were also important from a practical point of view, because they were employed to keep away rats who ate the silk worms which were very valuable to the Chinese, and even a cat painted on the wall of a room where silkworms were kept was thought to be a very powerful charm.

The Japanese kept statues of cats by the front door of their restaurants, both for good luck and to ward off rodents. The Japanese also believe you can cure a spasm by having a black cat put on the belly of a sick person. As the Romans have been given the credit for introducing cats into Britain they were, interestingly,

probably under the impression that they were doing us a favour—as, indeed, they were—because to them the animal was a symbol of liberty. The Goddess of Liberty was depicted holding a cup in one hand, a broken sceptre in the other and with a cat lying at her feet. The Romans also considered cats to have supernatural powers, including that of the Evil Eye: when they passed a cat in the street they nodded for good luck.

Other countries have customs totally repugnant to anyone who loves animals or, indeed, who has any regard for them at all. I, for one, can't visit Spain any more because they

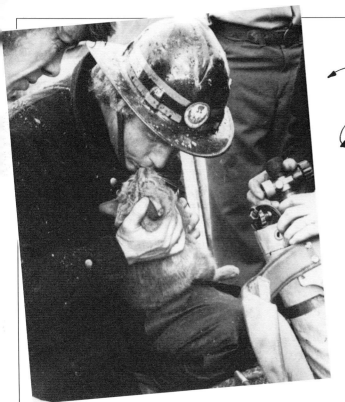

A life saver in New Zealand

Dutch Pussies Galore

treat animals so badly—cats in particular—and I'm so upset that people who visit the country go to the trouble of feeding them then have to leave them when they go home so the cats have to continue to run in packs to protect themselves and to try and scavenge such odd scraps of food as they can find near restaurants or in alleys or on dumps. It's the same in Portugal—they're just left to rot and die and nobody looks after them at all, except some-times well-to-do people in the big cities.

There's certainly no question in these countries of their being protected by the law—unless some recent developments, please God, have taken place—and dogs have no more rights there than cats. Eric Braun, my Press

Agent who has done a lot of cycling in both countries for years, finds it deeply distressing to pass literally hundreds of sad corpses of both species on the roads—on a bicycle you're going so much slower and can see the poor animal from almost a mile off, getting closer and closer, so you have to turn your head away as you go past. I have much admiration for what King Juan Carlos has done for Spain in the past ten years or so—while I write he is paying a State visit to our Queen in London—and if I ever had the perhaps unlikely honour of being presented I would have to say a word on the subject of animal welfare—protocol or no protocol.

I can't visit any of the countries where cats

So cats don't like water – eh?

What will they think of next? A cat goes hang-gliding in California

are treated badly by almost everybody and where the children are taken out to dinner at eleven o'clock at night with little wax faces and tiny little gold earrings in their ears and I think have almost as poor an upbringing as cats and dogs—but that's just my opinion.

California, on the other hand, seems to have gone to the opposite extreme. In 1973 the then Governor, Ronald Reagan, signed a bill into state law that can send a person to prison for kicking or injuring another person's cat— why is it always 'another person's cat', I wonder: some most definitely need protection from their owners, who surely have a prior duty to look after and care for their own. In that state, too, there are a number of absolutely

riveting amenities for cats, including their own acupuncturists, a cat resort, a feline rest home, a cat department store, a rent-a-cat agency, a pussycat dating service, cat psychiatrists, also feline acting courses and an annual meowing contest, which I think we can very well do without.

Holland, surely one of the most civilised European communities, treats the cat with respect, and again, there the animal has always been a symbol of independence: the Dutch used it on their banners in their struggle with Spain, who evidently did not take it as a hint to look after their own animals.

The countries where cats are kept as pets in almost as great a number as dogs are the

United Kingdom, Germany and Sweden, where they rate just one per cent lower in number than the dog population. Spain and Portugal, hardly surprisingly, come nowhere and in the USA there are just a little over four per cent less cats than dogs.

Cats have, of course, always been surrounded by superstition, which must have a bearing on the switchback nature of their fortunes. The Russians have an especially charming superstition, that if you want to be happy in a new home a cat must move in with

If you want to be happy in a new home a cat must move in with you.

you, and when you bring a new cat or kitten into your home, you must throw it on to your bed—mine don't need throwing, they're there anyway!—and if he begins to wash himself and settle down on the bed he will stay with you.

I've already mentioned the custom of buttering their feet which, in fact, is said to have originated in Europe, as a method of making sure they stay with you. France was another country where a cat was a symbol of liberty, for the French Revolution of 1789.

The superstition that was at the root of all the trouble of the Middle Ages must be the one where, for a time, all cats were believed to be the familiars of witches and witches were thought to have the power to turn themselves into cats to carry out their evil intentions.

It is said to be unlucky to hear a cat crying before you set off on a journey. If it does you are advised to return and find out what it wants. Well, you would, wouldn't you? That is just plain good sense and basic humanity. The other side of the witch theory rather favours the cat: according to East Anglian lore a witch who once called up a storm, which destroyed the fishing fleet, is said to haunt the fleet in the shape of a cat, which is why, to this day, sailors throw a little bit of their catch back into the sea 'for the cat.' Some might think that a waste of good fish, or perhaps just doing the fish a favour.

Some of these superstitions are just plain silly. How about the Welsh one that those who feed cats well will have sun on their wedding day? Or the one about the neighbour's cat: if your neighbour's cat comes round for a visit and sits listening, it's a sure sign that your neighbour is gossiping about you and that the cat will take home tales. My cats have far better things to do. If there were any truth in the old Chinese belief that a cat washing its face means a stranger is coming, I feel that Honeypot Cottage would be positively overrun with strangers which, happily to date, is not the case.

At harvest time in France a cat is decked in ribbons and flowers and cornstalks, as a symbolic form of sacrifice to the goddess of the harvest, as the cat is so closely associated with fertility—a nice thought, which I expect the animal appreciates. On the other hand, in earlier days in France, as well as in Russia, a cat was actually sacrificed and buried in the fields before the grain was sowed.

PRACTICAL ATTITUDES

Attitudes to cats and their care are universal in countries where they are well regarded, and, with the possible exception of the butter on paws, which seems to work anyway, have little to do with superstition—just plain common sense and learning from experience. Contrary to what people ignorant of their habits say, cats very rarely make messes indoors. Most of them will suffer considerable discomfort, if anyone is stupid or inconsiderate enough to leave them shut up for hours, before they will give way to doing their business where they know they should not. If this happens it's your own fault, and the only thing to do is to clear up as quickly and as thoroughly as possible, being careful to make sure no pong remains, which could, in the early days of training at least, lead your pet to think it would be acceptable to use the same place again.

It's amazing how easy kittens are to train, and in one day, if you put their front paws in their clean litter tray they will always go on that tray for ever after. Footy and Fred, if they were playing in the garden, would always break off to dash inside and use their tray. The tray, incidentally, must be kept clean; they will not be happy to use a soiled tray and there is no excuse for putting them to that inconvenience. If, in the early days, you see them settling anywhere else to do naughty messes they should be scooped up quickly and put on the litter box, but, if an accident should

happen—and, after all, cats are only human—they must be spoken to seriously and firmly, NEVER NEVER smacked or they will develop a phobia about the whole business of going to the loo and their natural training could be set back a long time, as they will be frightened and confused.

Four little meals a day are what kittens need, with water always nearby—perhaps milk mixed with a little water is preferable at that stage to plain milk. Always remember, that they are very bright from the word go and give them credit for that. The whole question of cat diets is an individual one—cats, like their owners, are totally individual and it is a case of both getting together to work out what is suitable and preferable to each pet. The various brands of tinned cat food have to subscribe to high standards of nourishment value and I'm sure they nearly always do, but they are by no means what every cat cares to eat as a steady diet. If they do, fine—otherwise, as Charles Kingsley, the author of that touching children's book *The Water Babies*, said, 'There are more ways of killing a cat than choking her with cream.' Only I'd say 'of keeping her alive.'

I will tell you my own experience of feeding my lot at Honeypot. With so many cats we do, of course, get through a mountain of food each week. In the olden days my mother used to feed Jumbo and Hamish on boiled lights—they are still available from some butchers for those who like them—but mine simply won't eat them.

Some of mine have tinned food, though I make sure to vary the kind from day to day, because, like us, there must be nothing more boring than eating the same thing day after day. Forget what Arthur the TV cat did—it has very little to do with what real cats are about, and he, poor love, certainly had to suffer, if not for his art, then certainly for his wages. I have two dozen tins of Whiskas a week, besides the minced lambs' kidneys, ox kidney and lambs' hearts which I keep in the freezer. Seven boxes sometimes go before the end of the week.

Some of mine have fresh meat—one day a week is mincing day, when Chris, who helps me and who has learned that cats can be every bit as interesting as dogs, minces up the offal that I think is so good for them and which they seem to enjoy so much. We give them mainly hearts and kidneys, which they like best, but avoid liver because it does tend to give animals diarrohea. The butcher's bill every week is pretty large, but he always sees we get the best available for the tribe.

My three year olds, Billy and Clive, took to red meat at an early age, which was a bit of a blow as it's so expensive to buy. Ronnie likes it too, but the five year olds won't eat meat at all—and none of them eats fish, except on sufferance, which is not as strange as you might think, in view of the commonly held belief that all cats dote on fish. This simply isn't true—if

My Clive, who acts as well as Clive Frances

they have a diet of fish it is extremely bad for their skin and fur. You see, our pets belong to the Big Cat family—panthers, pumas, lions, tigers and so forth—who are very much meat eaters, so it's not strange at all, when you come to think of it.

A special treat is cooked rabbit, which is Ronnie's hot favourite, and when I can get to Berwick Market I bring them back a rabbit or some fresh legs of rabbit: what is left over goes on the lawn for the foxes at night. I am very proud of my little animal kingdom and will repeat here what I said in my first book: 'happily the foxes get on very well with the cats, and I see them sitting in circles. When it's very cold I buy those fatty cheap breasts of lamb and cook them in the oven and put them on a great big dish or a tray outside, and there is a truce between all the animals when food is short. I've seen water rats, seagulls, my cats, ordinary little birds, voles, mice all eating together. There is no fighting: to me that is like having my own game reserve.'

not all of them, and they all have their different favourite things. They love hare which I have managed to get for them quite recently, but that's because it's gamey.

I am maddened when people say, or there are reports in the papers of some particularly violent or bad behaviour, 'They're just like *animals*'—they are not and never could be like animals, whose behaviour is perfect according to their natures; those who kill only kill to eat and they are quite incapable of getting up to the vile tricks of which humans are capable.

They can, however, be naughty, mischievous or even greedy, as I found to my cost during my stay in Africa. My friend John Boulter, who was in the show with me, had a wonderful big black girl servant called Letty. She was pure salt of the earth and a very great character, with immense courage, in her own right. She was also a great cook with a recipe for fish pie that was out of this world. One Saturday evening Letty had cooked a leg of lamb and left it out for John and myself to eat

They are quite incapable of getting up to the vile tricks of which humans are capable.

They like gamey things and if I ever have pheasant then my life's not really my own, because they do cadge when they smell something gamey. They rather like sharing—they like to think they're having something that belongs to you. Some of them like cheese, but

when we came home ravenous after two performances.

When we got there the cupboard was not only bare, but all that was left was a bone, picked clean. The cats, Anthony and Cleopatra, had got there before us. Ratty though we were, John said nothing to Letty in front of me, but the next morning I saw him walking round the garden with her, talking very seriously. She came in later to apologize. She said, 'Mr. Boulter says I have to say I'm a little bit disappointed!' So had I been, but I was also more than a little bit amused by the way she put it, considering a whole leg of lamb had been involved!

Some cats do have their exotic and strange tastes in food, to put it mildly. The things that they have been known to enjoy include asparagus tips, cantaloupe melon, chocolate, which most dogs adore but not so many cats, waffles (I must say I've not tried mine with those), corn on the cob, cheese (that's not too unusual, I think), soft-boiled egg, scrambled egg on toast, marzipan, Christmas cake, raisins, orange segments, custard skin, olives, mango and avocado, which, of course, we have come across before in this story. Others have liked peanuts (shelled, presumably) and baked potato skin; some of them also like to eat the potato itself,

I was her sister and down-to-earth and rather domesticated—she was frightfully grand and sophisticated with lovely clothes and a haughty manner, on stage I hasten to add, because off she's one of the dearest and most unpretentious people it's possible to meet. One of these books, Richard Graham's *Cuisine For Cats*, is absolutely riveting. On the cover is an intense black cat sitting in front of a bottle of Tomato Catsup, with a plate of fish with lemon and petits pois at its feet.

I quote one of a number of succulent recipes with which the author suggests you might like to tempt Puss—either in or out of Boots. He explains: 'Supposing that your own cat has committed the dastardly act of nobbling some friendly bird in the garden and has hopefully dragged it into the kitchen for you first to admire and then cook.' These little tokens of affection are one of the hazards of being a cat lover. 'You will first give it a homily on the unkindness of such behaviour, and the next thing is to dispose of the corpse. If you bury

Mary Shelley once asked her husband to come into the garden to watch their cat eating a rose.

cooked, with the skin on it. And Mary Shelley, wife of the poet and author of 'Frankenstein', once asked her husband to come into the garden to watch their cat eating a rose.

Siân Phillips was always bringing me books as a present when we were doing *Gigi* together.

it in the garden the cat will only watch where you have put it and dig it up again as soon as your back is turned: the waste disposal grinder is too cruel: the dustbin callous, though cremation, if you have an open fire, is feasible.

'But why waste food in a starving world?

Do as the Italians do. Pluck the little bird, impale it on a skewer, brush it with olive oil, salt and pepper, add a bayleaf and a few mixed herbs and roast it on the spit of your rôtisserie.' Eh? 'I would not advise serving it on a bed of Polenta, as the Florentine restaurateurs do, since cats prefer a starch-free diet, and this applies to serving it on triangles of fried bread as well. Just serve it up as it comes off the roasting spit.'

What a lovely idea, but a little bit of a tall order if you have ten pussies, as I once said to the obscene phone caller. Mr. Graham's book is full of rather less simple recipes, like the pigeon pie (one per cat), stuffed with its own chopped livers (the pigeon's I mean) and cooked in a pie dish with strips of puff pastry on top of small pieces of good stewing steak

(about 8 oz per cat.) That's all—quite simple, really, except you must not forget to place the halved bird on top of the steak, insides upwards and between them put sliced yolks of hard-boiled eggs. A little grated nutmeg, gelatine to form a jelly if you wish to serve it cold, some veal stock and the lid rolled out from your surplus pastry, decorated with cat motifs of your choice, bake for two and a half hours, and there you have it—a dish fit for a cat. Or a king, if one happens to be on your visiting list.

I can't wait to try that one Saturday evening after two performances. Or perhaps my readers would try it for me and let me know their cats' reactions. Could it be that Richard Graham is having a little game with us, and that secretly he believes his recipes are suitable for human consumption too?

South view of
a cat heading north

My Cat Owner Friends

When you become older—I nearly said when you get as old as I, but that sounds awful!—you don't expect to make new friends, but I have been so fortunate in having met Siân Phillips during the run of *Gigi*. She is such a strong character, such a wonderful person; I feel much richer for having met her and for knowing her and I'm sure our friendship will go on like Eileen Atkins and I—we don't speak sometimes for a year. But we will continue to be friends always.

SIÂN PHILLIPS

Siân has three Burmese cats, and they're all different colours, which is extraordinary. I have one little lodger who comes in whom I call Mountbatten, because he's almost the Star of Burma, but he's rather scatty and tries to disguise himself as Dimly and lie on a basket on top of the wardrobe. But Siân's are proper Burmese cats and she loves them: I hand over here to her to tell you about them—I know that her stories will be of great interest to all cat lovers. Strangely enough, we have worked together before without ever actually meeting, most recently in the film *The Doctor And The Devils*—but that's how it is with filming—if you have no scenes together often you don't meet.

My lovely new friend Siân surrounded by her cats

*M*y father didn't like cats—we always had dogs. I was born on a farm in South West Wales, so I've always lived with animals and was brought up in the country. In fact I was reared as a child by a black Labrador—he was kind of a nurse to me. He was a dog who had been an under-graduate's dog at a university and he had come down with my brother: he (the dog, I mean!) used to go and get all the drunks out of the pub and take them home, so for him a baby and a toddler were relatively easy, I imagine. He died when I was five and I'm afraid I can't remember his name. Not only did I not have cats, but they were not allowed in the house—to this day they're not allowed in the house in Wales. There was a lovely cat down on the farm when I went to visit with some friends and I asked my little niece, 'What's her name?' She, being about six, looked at me in amazement and said 'Cat!'

So it was wonderful when I was finally able to have cats: I had some in London when I even walked up the path to get in the car. There he was, this wonderful blue Burmese, who had talked all the way up in the car from Essex, where my husband had gone to get him. Unfortunately for me, he thought my husband was his mother, so I lost out a bit on him. Spencer is his name and I'm even now in the queue for his affections—I worship him, but Robin is the one he turns to and Spencer really behaved in a most bizarre fashion for weeks on end, quite convinced that my husband was his mother. I would have loved to have been his mother—or even his father, but he obviously didn't think I came into it at all!

I think it was really smart of me not to call him Joey, because if the play had come off in a week it would have been terrible to be lumbered with a cat called Joey. So he became Spencer, because although Burmese are very amusing, witty and funny there's something rather grand about them too, so it's a good name for him. Unfortunately, he's now quite

Spencer really behaved in a most bizarre fashion for weeks on end, quite convinced that my husband was his mother.

I settled here, but my last wave of cats, as it were, are the ones who've been closest to me. I have three Burmese and I was given my first ever Burmese in 1979 as a first night present for *Pal Joey*, the musical.

I came out of rehearsal one day and my husband Robin Sachs was standing there and I knew there was an animal in the car before

deranged—I really think he is mad, although he's quite happy in his madness, I'm sure.

The next year we decided we had to have another, so we got another brown Burmese called Barnaby. Spencer dropped my husband as a mother and became a mother to the new little boy, looked after him, walked him, saw he didn't go next door where there was a dog

Spencer and Rupert.

and really looked after him beautifully. When Barnaby went missing one day, Spencer was as distraught as I was and kept coming up to me and hitting me, looking in cupboards, patting cupboard doors to make me open them for him, but Barnaby wasn't there. He's the talker—he never stops. It was just awful— I've never seen an animal suffer so much.

Robin and I flyposted 500 bits of paper in our search for Barnaby and we walked all over Islington. Three weeks later I found him, in N19, which was miles away. He had a fractured leg and a gash on his forehead and he was so thin he looked like an Indian cow—you know, concave, as it were, no flesh at all. He had been abducted and locked away in a house and had worn away all the fur on his forepaws and all his claws were gone. He had fought like a tiger to get out and get home, and the woman, in the end, whose name I never took because I thought I might have killed her, had phoned the Cat Protection League in N19. They came to fetch him and had to pick him up with a remote control device—he was so ferocious they could not pick him up by hand. They took him to their Headquarters and couldn't even put him with the other cats. Burmese talk, but he's a silent cat. When they said, 'He could be yours—he's brown, and hasn't stopped shouting since he got here.' I thought, 'No—that can't be Barnaby but I'll have to go and have a look.'

Off I went with my cat box in the taxi and with every mile that I went I thought he could never have come all this way—it's impossible. When I got to the Cat Protection League, they told me, 'We've had to segregate him—he's out in the corridor on his own in a cage—we couldn't put him in the run in the back, he's too ferocious. I said, 'That's not my cat—it can't be—he's so young and so small.' I went out there—saw his one proud claw—and I realized it *was* Barnaby. He stopped talking and has never talked since. Nor has he grown since.

I took him home and he had a bandage on his leg and looked and smelled so appalling that Spencer who'd been pining all this time, turned on his heel and walked away! Barnaby is again perfect—he's absolutely wonderful; sleeps in the bed like all the others, but he doesn't like to be confined—he's always terrified of being locked up.

In the interval I'd got Spencer another baby—a blond one called Rupert (Rupert is called after a blond friend of ours—Rupert La Plante Sachs), so he was in the house and Spencer had adopted the baby. I thought it was going to be dreadful. They fight terribly but they play a lot and they sleep all wrapped up together and the three colours together are so wonderful. I think I must now have a lilac Burmese—that would be a wonderful addition to this range of colours.

My three cats are out of control—the whole house is geared to them: we're not allowed to shut any interior door because they simply take the carpet up if they can't get through. They sleep in the bed and go in and out of the cat door all night—I shudder to think what the laundry thinks we do to our sheets, because it's a sea of mud some nights. If they go in and out a lot all you get are little black pawprints.

They are completely impossible: they join us for food, either on a chair or sitting on the table. We're complete hypochondriacs about the cats, terribly worried they might get ill, so very often they're on bland diets like boiled chicken or boiled fish. They eat everything we eat—they like olives and a little bit of our meal on a side plate, besides some tinned food which is very highly recommended as a basis, because it's very balanced. When Robin carves the joint he carves for them first, and whenever they look off colour, which seems to be reasonably often—I'm sure they're fine, it's just that we worry about them—they go on their bland diet again. They love toast—toast and jam—so after they've had their breakfast they come in and have a bit of ours. They like eggs, fish pie—anything and everything.

Spencer is six, Barnaby four and Rupert about three and a half. I talk to them all the time. We had a dinner party for some people who don't know us very well and obviously didn't know we were mad about cats and it was going very well and we were chatting away and when I'm saying something I very often turn around and say, 'Isn't it Spencer?' or 'What do you think?' I could see my husband across the table was shaking his head very imperceptibly. We went on and the three cats were about, joining in the conversation from time to time, as it were, and everything, I thought, was going fine. But then Robin got up to take something to the kitchen and muttered under his breath as he passed behind me, 'Don't talk to the cats . . .!' Apparently our guests were going slightly boss-eyed: they couldn't believe that anybody was actually talking in that way to cats! But Burmese have to have conversation.

I miss my three so much. When I'm in a play, if Robin is away on a job, filming or in a play himself out of town, I never go out to supper, I go straight home—I have to see the cats. I think Rupert now thinks of me as his mother, and Spencer has accepted me as a good friend. He has also developed some dreadful habits which are really not printable—let's say he goes around 'marking', a squirt here and a squirt there, and leave it at that, except to say that it's completely odourless and colourless!

I once had a bulldog called Scobie, after Scobie Breasley: bulldogs are supposed not to be able to jump, but Scobie could leap fences and was a most unusual dog. He was sent away once to be trained with all the Alsatians. He was devoted to a wonderful kitten I had called Sherpa, who was a climber. Scobie used to soft-mouth Sherpa—pick him up in his mouth and carry him around, then when the baby was a little bigger he would get up on Scobie's forehead—a bulldog's forehead is so massive and they would walk around the garden and around the house with the kitten perched on the forehead of the bulldog and that was very touching. They used to sleep together and they absolutely adored each other.

I think if a kitten is introduced into a household which already has a dog it's a good thing, because the dog becomes very protective of the little thing. Scobie had never met a cat before this: he actually thought he was a cat. He was enormous but he used to climb on to one's lap and sit there comfortably, watching television. He loved rice pudding and spaghetti; bulldogs' mouths are very loose on the sides and the spaghetti used to fall out both sides!

I believe you have to put up with all this because I don't see why one shouldn't fit in with animals. People do sometimes say, 'Oh, that's really feeble—the house is for you and your animals should fit in with the way you live,' but I don't see why. I've had nicer times with animals than with a lot of people!

That's dedication for you and I must say I know exactly how she feels. I'm interested in the story about the bulldog and the kitten, because I'm often asked about how a dog might react to a new cat or vice versa and I just have no experience to go on. Maybe the answer is that it should be a kitten, rather than a fully grown cat, or a puppy rather than a grown-up dog.

What a lovely pair!

EILEEN ATKINS

Eileen starred with me in the play *The Killing Of Sister George* and we played a year and five months in London and seven months in New York. During all this time she didn't have a cat. When she came back she bought a big house with gardens in Camden Town and she acquired a cat, Finnegan. Then she got two more little ginger kittens, persevered in trying to get Finnegan to accept them, and, perhaps unwisely, on getting back from filming *Smiley's People* in Paris, moved to a flat which she found far from ideal. So she decided to move home again. Like Siân, she obviously thinks it's fairer to try to fit in with animals than to force them to fit in with you.

She now lives in a lovely house on the river between Kew and Chiswick and the cats again have a garden to play in, besides a smashing view of the river. In fact, her whole life has been switched round by cats. She's one of my favourite people—terribly funny and warm and such a superlative actress; I take my hat off to her in every way. She rang me up one day and said, 'I don't know what to do—Gus is being so awful to the kittens!' So I said, 'Just go to the pictures and when you come back you will see how many are left!' This sounds rather harsh, but it's the only way to cope with it, because they have to sniff each other out and the pecking order has to be established. They have to do it for themselves; you can't choose a leader for cats. I think now they're very happy, and I've asked her to talk about her cats.

*T*he first time I realized there were cats in the world, I think, was when I worked with Beryl and she used to start talking about her cats all the time. I thought she was a little bit crazy at first—she was always rushing back to see her cats and when we went to America she was desolate without them and used to ring up all the time to see how they were. I was so fond of Beryl by that time that I totally accepted that there was this woman who was mad about her Honeypot full of cats.

I always ring Beryl whenever I have any animal queries. I'm absolutely terrified of birds—cannot be near or handle them in any way. Her most riveting advice on how to handle a bird when you've got it away from a cat is to wrap it in a handy pair of warm knickers!

My father hated cats, like Siân's, I hear, and I was given one dog that my sister took out and got killed. I vaguely knew that this was my fault as I should have been out with it instead of my sister. I felt very guilty that I hadn't looked after it properly, and I now think that if you can't look after them, you shouldn't have them. I wouldn't even have a pot plant, because I felt I don't look after things, I'm never at home—I'm always out and so I can't look after anything.

Then, eight or nine years ago a journalist came to see me to do an interview for *Cosmopolitan* and I happened to know that this journalist

Dearest Eileen and Bill

had been forced to interview me and hated actresses. We were both doing the interview as a favour to the editor of Cosmopolitan. She came to the house in Camden Town and right at the end of the interview I thought I'd done so badly, she got to the door and said 'You don't want a kitten, do you?' and I thought it would please her if I said I would take the kitten as she was obviously a cat person.

So I replied, 'Oh, yes—that would be lovely.' 'Well,' she said, 'you've got a big house here—you can obviously take in a kitten.' It was a huge house with two huge gardens because we had the garden next door as well.

I forgot about it, didn't say anything to my husband Bill, then six weeks later along came a little photograph of this minute scrap of kitten, saying 'Here is your kitten, waiting for you to collect.' I'd been married about eighteen months then and Bill said 'If you said you'd have it you'd better take it and look after it—you've *got* to start looking after things!'

We went to Sally's and there was this adorable scrap of cat and we took it back home. Then I began to feel very sorry for it as it was all alone. Everybody had said to me that cats were really all right on their own but when we went away for a couple of weekends, I thought the poor little thing was lonely. So Bill agreed to get another one. I wish we'd taken another

Finnegan and Archie

from the original litter; people have no idea how wonderful it is to have at least two. So we put our name down on the RSPCA list with Beryl's lady, Muriel Carey, and my osteopath's lady from the RSPCA. I said I'd got a passion for a ginger cat as we'd already got the grey and white tabby, Finnegan. In the meantime a friend who wanted to give me a cat for Christmas turned up one day with a British Shorthair three months old from Harrods, where it had spent all its life until then. It was a high pedigree cat, vastly expensive.

Finnegan, who was about three months old and had got used to being the only cat, took one look at this cat and went to kill it; it shot straight up the chimney and refused to come down. We finally got it down, very lovingly, having decided it was quite the wrong companion for Finnegan and took it back to Harrods, where they received it with delight— apparently there was an old lady who had

wanted it terribly. So the lady took it joyfully and all ended happily.

Then, the RSPCA lady from Wimbledon rang to say she'd been given a sad cardboard box of four kittens found in Brixton and they didn't know if any of them were going to live. By the time we got there two had died and the two remaining ones were pathetic. They looked hideous with filthy bottoms and hadn't even been weaned from the mother and the RSPCA were just trying to save them. We played with them for a bit and said we'd let them know. As we got to the door to leave, one of the tiny kittens staggered after us. He could hardly walk and was the one who turned out to be Gus, who was always the stronger of the two. He stood there and just gazed at us. As we got into the bar Bill, almost in tears, said, "Oh dear, these two are particularly revolting, and with all the other pretty cats that were there, these were the two that were on offer to us.' I said, 'But now the cat has looked at us as we left and staggered to the door after us there's no way we can't take them.' He said, 'No, *of course* not!'

After we had been to collect them, I rang Beryl and she told me, 'You separate them for a little while from Finnegan and then gradually open the door and let them into the other room.' Well, there were loads of rooms in Camden Town, so they were put in a whole basement flat, where they were adorable. Suddenly they were racing up and down the floor, loving it all—but Finnegan was as jealous as Othello. He couldn't stand it—he'd been King of the Castle and he started smelling down there furiously. The odd thing was that he never

Archie and Gus

went for Gus, he only went for Archie (as we'd named his brother).

When they finally met, Finnegan fell in love with Gus almost immediately: they looked and loved but he always went for Archie. He beat Archie up until I could take it no longer: I rang Beryl one day and told her, 'I don't think I can bear it any more—I don't think he's going to take it.' 'Don't worry,' she said, 'I had the same trouble with Elsie when I got her home from Bristol. In the end I picked her up

other two, and he has become most peculiar, because he will only be cuddled on the bed. He won't be picked up at all—as I come in the door at night he'll go, 'Miaow, miaow, miaow—I want to go up to the bed.' Then he'll shoot up here and jump on the bed, and sometimes Finnegan gets very jealous and tries to get him off the bed.

There's this great jealousy: I sometimes have the terrible feeling that you do transfer your emotions to cats, and since I am myself

In the end I picked her up by the scruff of the neck and I said 'How d'you fancy a one-way ticket to the vet?'!

by the scruff of the neck and I said 'How d'you fancy a one-way ticket to the vet?'! I picked up Finnegan and I said the magic words—she's absolutely right; it takes about two weeks.

Finnegan still duffs up Archie, he doesn't like him but he keeps it within limits. But the love affair that goes on with Gus is beyond belief with the result that Archie has become a terribly strange cat. Finnegan and Gus lie in each other's arms—it's really beautiful to watch, and poor Gus is between everything. He's trying to keep Finnegan happy and yet he's very fond of his brother and he's always going up and giving little pats, then he'll sometimes take a swipe at Gus because he's gone off with Finnegan. The emotional relationship between them is incredible, so we've given Archie a great deal more fuss and love than the

a violently sexually jealous woman I think I passed it all on to the cats!

This is how I sum up my own cats: Finnigan is the most touchy and a bit difficult; if you don't stroke him first when you come in he'll take against you. He should come first. Gus has absolutely everything—he's the prettiest, the one that the others both love, he's the bravest, the most curious and I'm sure it's all because he *is* loved by everybody. He'll sashay up; he goes up and down the Strand, goes visiting. Archie is the plainest, always being beaten up by Finnegan, whines all day, wanting different things. Actually, Archie is a pain in the arse, but I love him absolutely as much as the others. It's been a great lesson to me that, like people, just because they're ugly and a pain in the arse it doesn't stop you loving them!

I did, in fact, soon after this, get a letter from Finnegan. It read:

Dear Beryl,

I'm so sorry I'm not looking my best in this photograph, but if some idiot came up behind you and shouted 'Look at me, Finnegan' and let off a flash-bulb at you, you wouldn't be looking your best, either. Of course they spend hours posing—the other two—'Oh, aren't they sweet—quick, take one of them now'... 'Ah, look, they're cuddling each other!' Honestly, Beryl, it makes you sick.

And then they try to make out that they had them as company for me. Well, if they'd given me any choice I wouldn't have chosen two scruffy-looking gingers from No Fixed Abode. Well—a cardboard box on a rubbish tip in Brixton—I don't call that any address. After all I come from Islington and my mother's owner was a well-known journalist. Her home was a bit Bohemian, but very arty and upper-crust. They should have found me companions with the same interests and outlook as myself—not Rough Trade.

I like sitting rather disdainfully amongst the cushions and rugs that enhance and harmonize with my colourings. You understand that, Beryl, of course—there's very little that doesn't suit me. Well, dark grey tabby looks well with everything, but ginger doesn't go with much. Sometimes I sit in the window bay being admired by passers-by, occasionally giving the ducks a bit of a fright, and sometimes I have a nifty game with a paw cork (yes, well, there are plenty of corks in this house, Beryl) and I am a superb dribbler and pat a cork around with smartly fancy paw work.

When she threw the cork down for me to show off a bit in front of the other two, Archie—he's the really dumb one—took it in his mouth and ran off with it and she thought it was funny. Oh, yes—laughed and laughed—had a bit too much bubbly, of course, so I went and hid for a bit—that always puts the wind up her.

A couple of hours later it was 'Finnegan, Finnegan— Where are you, darling?" But what am I going to do with these other two, Beryl? They're tearing about the place with no dignity: they're very pushy and bad-mannered about food, and, honestly, they'll eat anything. I mean, standards here will go down if they think they can get away with tinned food morning and evening. You see, I do like a little bit of fresh coley, poached chicken or liver in the evenings.

I hold out some hope for Gus: I noticed he was copying how I sat on the wall outside and didn't let just anyone stroke him. I think I might make a cat out of him eventually. But Archie—well, he has the most common miaow and rolls on his back for anybody. I saw him sniffing the flowers: actually, Beryl, I'm a bit worried he might be a bit of a woofter—you know what I mean Beryl—displays his feelings far too obviously; more like a dog in that respect. Need I say more?

I hope you're keeping well, Beryl, getting the cream and keeping your fur clean.

Your fond friend,
Finnegan

More Cat Owner Friends

One of our most gracious actresses and perhaps one of the gentlest people in the world was Anna Neagle. I didn't know her very well, but I often met her on state occasions like the *Night of 100 Stars* and the Royal Variety Show, when we shared a dressing-room. Occasionally we would meet at a party, like the one which a friend of ours, Fergus Montgomery, gave at the House of Commons out on the veranda. She was always very quietly spoken, very gentle and greatly to be admired for all the wonderful work she did in films. My own personal memory of her goes back to the war, when she was one of the stars I used to do impressions of.

She, too, was a great cat lover, and, I know, had a tale to tell. Her secretary-companion, Joyce Wright, who had been with her for years and was often her cat-minder when Anna had to be away working, told me about the dozens of cats that inhabited her dressing-room— though not at the Royal Show, I hasten to add. They were not real ones, of course, but china ones, glass ones, wooden and stuffed ones in a variety of shapes and sizes. Joyce added, 'If there's one thing she loved more than the theatre, to which she was dedicated, then it was cats.' Here is Anna's own story about one of her favourite cats:

I was living in Brighton and doing a very long tour of a thriller called *Person Unknown*, which stretched over two years, with interruptions, between 1963 and 1965, when Tuppence came into our lives. My husband, Herbert Wilcox, and I had gone through a bad patch financially, and that play came as a godsend to help us through our difficulties; though the touring was hard work. The first few months took me to places I'd never played in before and I was able to meet and stay with old friends I'd had little opportunity of seeing previously. The brightest spot of all this period was Tuppence, who walked into our lives through the garden window one summer evening, a small, determined beautiful ball of fire and fur. She accepted a morsel of food and then disappeared.

We decided she had been abandoned, and, in view of her large waistline, not only abandoned, but abandoned pregnant. Later we discovered that this was just a myth. She was, in fact, plain greedy, and an actress to boot, knowing exactly how to manipulate human beings around her little paw. She had large, golden eyes that could melt your heart, then turn to the dark thunder of sudden anger. She was 'all cat' and wouldn't have thanked me for describing her as almost human, which is a fairly insulting thing to say, when you come to think of it. She wasn't everybody's cat, either; she liked or disliked, and it worked in reverse.

It was weeks before we discovered she had a perfectly good home of her own, and in the meantime we'd scoured the neighbourhood in vain, and when no one owned up to knowing her we congratulated ourselves on having befriended so beautiful a creature. How could anyone have abandoned her? With this in mind we encouraged her when she appeared, which was every day. Apart from refusing milk she steadily and daintily ate her way through all that was offered. This cat's motto seemed to be 'anything you can eat I can eat,' besides

Dame Anna, Tuppence I and Ginger Rogers

devouring the vitamin pills I kept providing for her purely phantom pregnancy.

We were walking in the gardens, when a voice cried, 'There's Tuppence—what are you doing out here?' The owner of the voice was regarded with an icy stare and Tuppence began washing herself furiously: no wonder she'd not responded to any of the names we'd tried on her. We tried to sound sincere when we said, 'Thank goodness—we wondered where she had come from, but she looked lost and hungry and seemed to take to us.'

Then we heard the story—the *true* story of a well-cared for family pet, bred on a farm, whose family had moved to a flat in our part

After hearing all this we hardened our hearts and packed Tuppence off home, but it was a lost cause, at least for us. Day after day she came back and her pathetic performance at the window would have earned her the lead in *East Lynne*, or even *Stella Dallas*. Eventually, after mutual agreement with her owner it was decided she was to be adopted permanently by us.

She was, in some ways, a non-conformist to the habits of her species. Although she hunted, as was her nature, we never saw her 'play' with or torture her prey. Birds didn't appear to interest her. Mice and rats from the gardens were killed outright with a single blow. Once

We found it a wrench to leave the small face that always managed to be watching from the window as we left.

of the world, and who didn't much care for that. Furthermore, she did not see eye to eye with her son Whitesocks, who she obviously thought should have left the nest, but hadn't. He was timid and chaste—the exact opposite of his mother, whose secret life didn't bear investigating. No matter where she roamed, which turned out to be far and wide, she made a habit of returning home once a week to consume a good dinner and provoke Whitesocks to a round of fisticuffs. This inevitably ended in disaster and a box around the ears for him; his mother packed a lethal left hook.

dead, they were left, or, if the fancy took her, presented to the person of her choice. The only difficulty, then, was to dispose of the corpse without hurting her feelings.

When I went into the musical *Charlie Girl*, which was to run for more than five years at the Adelphi, Tuppence was, during the early days of the show, cared for during the week by friends in the neighbouring flat. But we found it a wrench to leave the small face that always managed to be watching from the window as we left. Our arrival back in Brighton each weekend was always greeted by an extremely sleepy but happy cat. A soft purr of welcome and she was back to bed. Tuppence had very strong views about bed. If we came home at all hours, that was our affair, but five minutes later she'd be fast asleep again, safely assured that we were back. In the end, we could stand the separations no longer and brought Tuppence to London.

Herbert Wilcox, my husband, was in New York on a business trip—he was fully restored to health, after a thrombosis which had blighted the Golders Green opening of *Charlie Girl*, his discharge from bankruptcy was well and truly behind us, and the world again a good place to live in—and since we didn't know what would be his reaction to having a 'London' cat, we chose that time to lead her into the car, complete with sleeping basket, cat litter, collar, lead and food. For the rest, we just had to pray that she was the cat we considered her—intelligent and adaptable. She never disappointed us. She didn't, of course, choose to sleep in the basket, regarded the cat litter as for *our* use and dug up the nearest rosebeds. The collar and lead she would never wear except under extreme provocation. We awaited Herbert's arrival with baited breath—and he greeted her with delight.

When we gave up the Brighton flat, Tuppence actually chose our new home. Naturally she came with us to view. The garden boasts the most beautiful hydrangea bush. She sat in the middle, flatly refusing to come out and using every tooth, claw and some quite unprintable language. It was either buy the lease—or the bush!

She loved, hated, played and was completely vulnerable to any harsh word. She fawned to no one, picnicked on Wimbledon Common and dined at the Savoy and, of course, came to the theatre. At the Adelphi she was always first down the stairs into my dressing-room. She saw the suitcases, which meant 'going away', and she always found out, no matter how surreptitiously we packed. She came to airports, oblivious of the noise around her, quite calm, to see us off. She flirted outrageously with the personnel—but could spot phoney 'cat lovers' a hundred yards off, and she'd never try to win a non-cat lover over to her side.

When I returned from a tour of Australia and New Zealand, Joyce Wright, my secretary, was there to meet me, but not my darling Tuppence. She'd been rather unwell and she thought that even Tuppence, the perfect airport cat, would perhaps get restless if there were any delay.

A year or so later I opened in *No, No, Nanette* at Drury Lane, and on the day before the first night Tuppence disappeared. We had been rehearsing all day and a preview at night. So I was not told until I got home. Joyce and Herbert had searched the entire neighbourhood, as I did the next morning. Sadly I had to leave for the theatre and the opening performance. In the first interval a call came through to my dressing-room. The small daughter of an actress living nearby had seen the Tuppence Missing notice. They had found her in their garden the previous night and taken her in. Mrs. Martin, who helps take care

Dame Anna on her eightieth birthday with Tuppence II: October 20 1984

of us at home, was with Joyce 'taking care' of our guests at the theatre. They dropped everything as soon as the curtain went up on the second act, grabbed a taxi, and when I came off at the end of the show Tuppence was safely curled up in her usual spot ...

For me there was a great sadness when Tuppence was again missing: once more the 'theatre' found her. Another theatrical family who, by happy chance, shared our vet, had taken her to him. We had known for some time that she was far from well and sadly he con-

firmed what we already knew deep down. She was frail and fifteen years old, or thereabouts. In my arms I carried her round the garden she so loved. That afternoon she died. She is buried in a small grave where rosemary is growing in profusion. But it's not necessary to call on the rosemary. Tuppence will never be forgotten: a small cat, with a vivid, brave and unforgettable personality. She was succeeded by Tuppence II, but, as Beryl said, you don't 'replace' cats—you just find room for another one of them in your heart.

ROBERT LUFF

Robert Luff I have already introduced to you in this book. It will come as no surprise that he is a lover of all animals, as all gentle people are. He has his own story to tell, and here it is:

*C*ats, dogs, rabbits and all animals were an important part of my earlier life. My late sister, who was quite a bit older than me had arranged in our barn at home in Bedford wired partitions for ailing animals and it was not infrequent to see either a dog, cat, bird or rabbit being brought back to health through her ministrations. My father used to refer to it as the infirmary and she had infinite patience and a way of handling animals when they were injured. One of her close school friends was the daugher of our vet and she used to ask her questions about the problems of the animals and in turn her friend would ask her father what treatment they should be receiving. This had been going on for some time when he mentioned to my father while playing bowls that it appeared he was giving a lot of his professional advice to his daughter and he had a sneaking suspicion it was ending up with my sister!

Our family lived in a crescent which was built up completely on one side and on the other side were allotments in which we used to wander. Living nearby there was an elderly lady who had a nice black and white tom called Rupert. He was well known to us all as a very friendly cat who used to wander about a bit but usually was sensible enough to go home for his meals. However, during the holiday absence of the housekeeper, the old lady was standing at her gate calling Rupert. When I came up and asked her what she was worried about, as I had seen him not far away, she said she didn't like him being out too long, so I volunteered to find him. Within about half an hour I discovered him in the bushes down the road and brought him safely home, to be greeted warmly and given tuppence for my trouble, which in those days represented at least a quarter of a pound of sweets and could only be described as a windfall.

The fellow members of my gang were surprised to see me so affluent at a time in the week when we were normally skint: when I told them the sources of my good fortune meaningful glances were exchanged, and within a few days the old lady was again seen at her gate seeking Rupert. Two of us went off to find him, which again was not very difficult as he was not far away. Needless to say we found him but we didn't want to bring him back too quickly,

so we took him to a hide-out for an hour and then went back to be rewarded with threepence. This went on for another week and the lady in question stopped my father at the gate, within my earshot, drawing his attention to my kindness and she also unfortunately mentioned in passing that I had received some remuneration.

My father's reaction was, 'Oh really, that is very interesting and I am glad the boy is helpful, but would you kindly refrain from giving him money in future, as I am sure he would be delighted to do it for nothing.' That same evening he said, 'You can go on finding Rupert and any other cats that are lost, but you will never take money.' He also expressed his puzzlement that Rupert should have been lost for so long as the last time, when we had received sixpence, we had secreted him for three hours to make our case the stronger. I don't think that my father, knowing the cat to be a wily old warrior, thought he would have missed his mid-day meal if he could help it. Thereafter, of course, it never took us longer than about 20 minutes to find Rupert!

My late partner Beryl was tremendously fond of animals and in her memory I founded the Beryl Evetts and Robert Luff Animal Welfare Trust (BERLAWT), which supports all animal charities: although she liked dogs she shared my view that a dog's life on the Earl's Court Road would be very short, as more human beings are lost on this road than crossing the Atlantic.

In the house next door over a weekend she saw a cat scraping on a window in a house which was apparently completely vacated. She managed to retrieve it the following day when its owner came back, and, having reprimanded her for leaving the cat unattended and unfed, volunteered to keep it and so Smiggy became a part of No. 294. When I came back from the Army in 1945, Smiggy was a well established part of the house. During the war when Beryl lived alone in the house, Smiggy was a great asset, because it had a cat's sixth sense of when a bomb was going to drop and would shoot under the table, quickly followed by Beryl. The house was blasted back and front, and when there was time she would go into the air raid shelter and not come out until Smiggy led the way, knowing that the danger had passed.

After Smiggy died I secured a beautiful cream pedigree Persian through my vet. He had sold this expensive cat to an American heiress called Mimi Medard, who became the Countess of Coventry: when I went to collect the cat the lady was quite sad about parting with her and asked whether I would be prepared to come back in a week's time when she

her passing had left: I went to Notting Hill to a lady who bred Persians and she showed me a litter of three—a cream, blue cream and black. The cream would be Honey II and I was rather taken with the blue cream who seemed to be a lively little party, so I thought I would take two of the three home for Beryl to choose from.

Needless to say that was fatal, because dear Beryl kept them both and immensely enjoyed their company for sixteen years; Smokey was Honey's companion, and during most of this time I had the *Black and White Minstrel Show* at the Victoria Palace. The girls used to come round for a cup of tea and see the cats, and every week when I went to the theatre they would always ask after Honey and Smokey. In their later life, when the cats were ailing, it always appeared that they would become ill between Friday afternoon and Monday morning when most of the vets are closed, and so over the last years of their lives I became familiar with every vet within a distance of ten miles of Earl's Court!

Over the last years of their lives I became familiar with every vet within a distance of ten miles of Earl's Court!

would be leaving London. I duly returned and brought back this lovely little animal which we named Honey and enjoyed her company until her death in 1963.

Honey had made us aware of the charms of this breed of cat and we felt we would like another of the same kind to fill the void which

Some four years ago my secretary left and Gillian Lindo, who has been with me for many years, was left to cope alone. 294 is a large house and it was suggested to me that I should advertise for a secretary who could live in and look after the house in my absence. I duly did this and received several replies. I interviewed most of the applicants and decided to offer the job to my present secretary, Rhonda. When she attended her second interview she said she had a slight problem as she had a cat which she would have to find another home for. Of course my interest was doubled, and she told me her cat was 'just a moggy', but lovely nevertheless. Rhonda moved in the following weekend.

After she had been here about one month I went away for the weekend on business and arrived back on the Monday afternoon to be confronted by two rather shy secretaries. When I asked what was going on, I was taken downstairs and when the bathroom door was opened a tiny little kitten came bounding out. I named her Sandy, because of her colouring, and although I refer to her as a nervous bag of bones, she has joined the other cat, Tweeky, in being part of a loving household at 294.

ERIC BRAUN

In 1968, my Press Agent, Eric Braun had a house-warming party at his flat. A lady called Miriam Maisel, who is a journalist and devoted to cats, had the care of a litter of kittens, who had been thrown with their mother from a moving car. I can think of no way of describing 'people' who will do things like that and no punishment too extreme to meet the case: the kittens survived and Miriam gave two of them to Eric because he couldn't have dogs when he lived in his flat. They were called Sid and Rene because those were the names of the characters Hugh Paddick and I were playing at the time in a TV series called *Wink to Me Only*.

It was a very swingy party—everybody was having a very good time, but, unfortunately the door had been left open and also the door of the flat across the way, and little Sid and Rene, only a few months old, who were in great shape when I arrived, had dashed across and fallen into a bucket of paraffin for cleaning paint brushes and so on, which did them no good at all.

Thank goodness I found them (I did

With kittens Rene (left) and Sid and Jess Conrad at Eric Braun's flat-warming party in Notting Hill Gate; August 1969

arrive with a tin of cat food, by the way, in case they needed some). I got them out, and washed them, poor little things, because I was afraid of their eyes being blinded. It's such dangerous stuff, really. I also scrubbed the floor around where the liquid had been split, just in case they ever got in there again. The little things were rubbed dry, purred and fell asleep.

Since then, they moved with Eric to live in Strawberry Hill. When Eric found two Basset Hounds from Basset Rescue they, Freddie and Honey, were very happy. But his cats were not: they did not see eye to eye or paw to paw, and one by one they emigrated down the road from 36 Michelham Gardens to No 52, where a lady called Margaret Woodward and her husband keep open house for needy animals. The first to go were Tom and Jerry, two wildly furry part Persians, and eventually they took Rene with them—Tom had departed this world some years before.

From being casual visitors and diners they decided to move in, bag and baggage. Margaret notified Eric, visiting rights were established, but they were not to be coaxed back. Only one cat, Toni, stayed, to become firm friends with the dogs. Her brother Cleo (names were switched when the sexes turned out to be the other way round) also moved to the Woodwards.

I had a touching letter from them as I was preparing this book:

Dear Miss Reid,
You will be pleased to know we still have one of Eric's cats—Tom of the Tom and Jerry pair. My

daughter re-named him Christopher as he is an unusual cat—very fond of birds, but not to eat. He has a sort of paternal instinct and collects up any little waifs and strays of birds when they are tiny, and sick, or fallen out of the nest, and gently carries them home to my husband— carefully negotiating the cat flap—and they always arrive uninjured. We have saved many, including a two-day-old pigeon which he gave to my husband on the Queen's Silver Jubilee—which we had the joy of seeing fly away at six weeks old—he was quite tame, and we taught him to fly in the garden. Christopher is often to be found in the garden with the birds pecking food all round him—at first we used to wonder if he was blind but now we know he is just unusual and very trustworthy.

He is now about 14 years old and very fit—definitely the boss of the other two cats and a special character. He permits no fighting or bullying among the cats and we think he would be irreplaceable.

With love and very good wishes for your next book

Thank you again Margaret Woodward

AUDREY SMITH

Audrey Smith, the journalist, is a great cat person and has recorded for me an account of her life with Sagittarius, or Saggi for short, in their flat in Putney:

*M*y life has never been the same since a day, ten and a half years ago, when I walked into the hut reserved for *cats* at Battersea Dogs' Home and saw a very young, pretty tabby kitten literally waving to me through the bars of its cage.

'I have to have that cat,' I said out loud and returned to my office at *Woman's Own* with an approximately six-month old, cost 57s 6d, who on arrival ate a whole tin of food, used the litter tray and posed for all the visitors from other departments. 'Such charm, such intelligence,' cooed Romany astrologer, Leon Petulengro. 'She's just like me, she's got to be a Sagittarian!' Well, so am I, but I don't claim to be marvellous, so the name stuck, though by virtue of her age she's got to be a Taurus or maybe Gemini or Cancer.

That night I asked a cab-driver if he could take us all the way to Putney and as we drove down Whitehall I pointed out all the buildings I felt she should know about. I said, 'And over there is Downing Street. The Prime Minister lives there,' and she was promptly sick all over the back seat (over-excitement, I'm sure). Apart from that she has never had a moment's sickness in her life—touching the wood of the wardrobe from which she likes to look down at visitors from a great height.

What a hope! I woke to the sound of pan lids being thrown around—she was on top of the kitchen cupboard and when she came down to earth she ate *two* pieces of cod for her breakfast. Though she has never had to go back to the vet's, one year Mr. Cameron came to give her a booster injection in the flat. Can you imagine the scene? He and I were standing on my bed, with Saggi poised on the wardrobe top. Then as she slid down the wall—woosh, in went the needle—no problem, and one cat immune for the year.

She likes my being a freelance, so I can sit with her most days and type my work, but she does look angry the nights I have to go off in the evening to Wardour Street screenings, 'No,' I tell her, 'though I go off to Soho I'm not a hooker—I just review films.' I don't think she believes me!

During hot summers she's treated like a

As she slid down the wall—woosh, in went the needle—no problem, and one cat immune for the year.

She had the one visit to the vet's, for her necessary op. 'Call for her tonight, Audrey.' they said, 'She'll be very sleepy for a couple of days and don't give her too much to eat.' I picked her up in the evening. She was dozy, looked at me reproachfully and then at her wound. 'How could you do this to me?' she said with her eyes.

I went off to sleep that night, thinking I wouldn't waken her too soon in the morning,

starlet at the Cannes Film Festival, with her miniature deck chair from 'Woolies' and me serving her at intervals with dishes of iced water. I always told Saggi, 'If I don't come back one day I'll be in hospital. If I live I'll be back.' Four years ago I had to go in, my kindly next door neighbour fed her night and morning, played with her in the evenings and when I walked back into my flat nearly four weeks later, a smiling cat rubbed round my legs, satisfied that the status quo was resumed—and no looks or expressions of reproach.

My first real outing after that was to go to a garden party in Strawberry Hill to celebrate Beryl's first twenty-five years of working with Eric. I pointed out the picture of Beryl with Footy on her lawn at Wraysbury and said, 'Look—I'll be all right—that lady adores cats'.

Mind you, Saggi takes a lot of convincing. One night I arrived home from a press reception at L'Escargot Restaurant, following the launch at Channel 4 of Bernard Levin's programme *Hannibal's Footsteps*. A copy of Mr. Levin's book had been given to me and on the first page is written 'To Saggi, with very good wishes, Bernard Levin.' Though she must be one of the few cats in Britain to own her personally signed copy, she was much more impressed with the Pacific prawns I'd brought back in my catty-bag!

TERRI HOWARD

When I went to Eric's party in Strawberry Hill in 1982 I met, for the first time since she had understudied me in *Mother Goose* in Brighton, many moons before, Terri Howard, who went on to become a notable Principal Boy and a notable cat lover. She lives in a lovely old cottage down the road from Strawberry Hill, on the Thames Embankment, with several very beautiful cats, mostly rescued from fates worse than death, and for this she has my admiration. She told me about the loss of one of her favourite cats of the past:

*I*t was the last night of *Dick Whittington* at Richmond Theatre, and sadly, that was the night my cat Lily died. She was a lovely old cat. I had a wonderful 'Cat' in the pantomine, who was Helen Worth, now, of course, in *Coronation Street*, but she couldn't make up for the loss of my Lily. Freddie Piffard, who then owned the theatre, was a great animal man and anti-vivisectionist and he knew how upset I was. He rang and said, 'I know of just the cat for you,' and I said, 'I can't have another, because I'm leaving to do a summer show.' But he insisted on driving me down to Shepperton to this Animal Rescue place, where I collected this lovely black Persian girl—a real Persian with the short legs and short body—and I didn't even have a basket, I was so sure I wasn't going to be persuaded, but in the car she put both arms round my neck and purred and sang and made it very clear that she was very happy. I called her Emma.

When I decided I was going to go away and take her to the Bournemouth Pavilion where I was doing my summer season, I asked the vet how I should travel her and he said, 'You'd better put her under tranquilizers.' I had her firmly tranquilized, and closed into a cat basket and everthing. The silly thing is that for the eleven or twelve years she travelled with me after that she used just to get into the car and never even had a basket. She was quite content to travel, sitting on my knee most of the time, often with the old poodle of my driver. My Emma would be on one knee, and Sally the old poodle, on the other. They were best friends until Sally died at the age of 17.

Terri Howard as Dick Whittington with Richmond Theatre cat Tabs II

Freddie then got two zebra finches, but it became too much—I don't think he could be bothered with them—and he asked me to have them. They're dear little birds but I said to Him 'You're taking a risk, because after all I've got to take a cat now, plus a bird cage, plus my small son Richard and all the paraphernalia of touring.' Anyway, Emma became very fond of these birds: she used to travel in the back of the car—it was a sort of station waggon—and she used to lean against the cage, so that her whiskers went through the bar, and the male bird used to stand on her whiskers!

Emma's first Christmas away was in Bournemouth—we had a nice flat on the East Cliff—it was Richard Todd's flat, overlooking the Isle of Wight, and she was quite content just to sit on the windowsill and watch the birds and use her own toilet in the bathroom. In the summer of 1979 when I did a summer season at Skegness—Richard, then at boarding school, came with me—I had a beautiful trailer caravan which I rented, right by the sea and I took the birds with me—Uncle Dee Dee and Dum Dum, his second wife—who were very happy having eggs all the time, which never matured, still they were a devoted couple. I have a photo of Emma sitting on a chair and the birds hanging above her head.

The next year she died and I swore that I would never, ever, have another black Persian, but my friend, who is a member of the Cat's Protection League in Bromley, rang and said, 'You've got to have this cat—she is the image of Emma.' I said, 'No'—and ended up with the thinnest cat that the vet said he had ever known to be still alive. She was found running in Croydon High Street with a three-week-old kitten in her mouth—and she was only a kitten herself. She was too ill to feed the kitten, which the League found a home for, and I took Daffodil, as she became, and had to feed her on cod and chicken. The moment she started to be better she saw Uncle Dee Dee hanging on the wall and leapt twenty feet and swung on his cage. It took a lot of persuading and introducing her before she became very friendly with him and never bothered him again.

A year later, by which she'd become a rotund Toblerone-shaped cat, I moved from Sheen to Twickenham, and one day, dumped in the next door garden, which was empty, I found a little tiny grey and white kitten, which took me two days to rescue. It had half of its tail missing and was covered in ticks: anyway, I left it in the cottage in the care of the builder when we did the move and Daffodil, on arrival, took one look, said 'My long-lost kitten,' went straight towards it and gave it a good wash. When I saw a picture of Daffodil at the time she was rescued, taken with her original kitten—it was uncanny how this one was the spitting image of that lost kitten. I called the arrival Kittone and he and Daffodil lived together very happily as mother and son, in each other's arms.

Next pantomine time—things always seem to happen to me then—I was at Peckham playing Fairy Godmother, and I opened my door and there, nestling on the door step, was this wonderful very very large male cat wearing a white collar. It was terribly cold with thick snow all around. He was black, with huge eyes and great big ears—like a small black panther. 'Where is Mr. Jackson?' he said. 'Well, you'd better come in,' I replied. Well, he was in by that time anyway and walked straight into the kitchen, had something to eat, then went into the toilet, used the litter tray—straight upstairs into my bedroom and into the airing cupboard and went to sleep.

I had to go to the theatre and didn't know quite what to do, so I told Daffodil and Kittone, 'Look after him, please and I'll be back at half-past eleven.' When I got back that night, in fear and trepidation, they were all together, as if they were one happy family. I never could find out where he came from—he was half Siamese and very intelligent—even though he was wearing a collar. I called him Booby, and he can communicate with me: one day he looked at me and he said, 'Dinky'. Ever since then Kittone's been called Dinky. To complete our family, last July my friend with the Cat Protection League in Bromley, who had had a bad accident and dislocated her back, asked me to come over and help her. She had this rescued cat in a pen—a black and white one who was crying: real tears were running down his face and splashing on to his chest! So I kept going over and looking after him for her and two weeks later, I brought him home and he became Russell. And a very happy family they all are.

My Favourite Cat Stories

And Poems From Around And About

We have looked into the lives of almost every known variety of cats, including Persians, Burmese, Siamese, toms, alleycats, Royal and Parliamentary cats, stage, screen and TV cats, literary cats, detective cats, working cats, dancing cats—a whole Dynasty of Honeypot cats, but not, so far any jet-setting cats. Today jet-setting would be impossible for cats because of the Laws of quarantine, but Mr. Fing flourished in the 'twenties and 'thirties, when what would now be called the jet-setting class travelled cosily, and at leisure, on ocean liners. He took centre stage on the great floating hotels and is alleged to have crossed the Atlantic 11 times.

THE STORY OF MR. FING

He was the most highly publicized cat of his day, and I would never have known about him if the writer Raye Virginia Allen had not come into my life while I was appearing in *Gigi*. I knew she had been in this country three times already, researching the life of one of the theatre and cinema's leading dress designers of the period, Gordon Conway, and I had promised to record something for her about cats to fit into her biography as Miss Conway—yes, she was a girl, because in her family they

International designer Gordon Conway
in the 'twenties with her jet-setting cat
Mr. Fing, né Soho Billy

christened girls with boys' names, and I don't know what Sister George would make of that—did her most important work for stage and screen here and in Paris.

We didn't meet until *Gigi*, because I had been caught up between *The School For Scandal* and the touring revue *A Little Bit On The Side* during Raye Allen's previous visits. She came to my dressing room, took some really smashing photos and brought what can only be described as her case history on Mr. Fing, which is a book in itself. The Americans are nothing if not thorough, and Raye, as a cultural historian from Washington D.C. is not only from the Deep South, but learning all she can about show business over here, and Mr. Fing was very much a part of that in his time.

From Soho to Sainthood is the title of his story—well, I don't know about that, but it's certainly a case of 'From Soho to Society.' The fascinating point about his rise to fame is that he started life as a Soho Alleycat, was taken in by the proprietor of the Chantecler in Dean Street and christened Billy. When Gordon Conway and her husband went there to dinner one night, Billy jumped down from his window seat to rub against her feet and purr, then climbed on to her lap. The love at first sight was mutual, and after more meals at the restaurant, the famous dress designer won her campaign to adopt Billy, whisked him off to live at Claridge's to become part of her life as an international celebrity and swapped the perfectly good name Billy for Mr. Fing, deciding that it had a good ring to it and that he probably had oriental blood in him anyway!

From then on he commuted between London, Paris, France and Paris, Texas, although crossing the Channel he had to suffer the humiliation of travelling on a dog ticket, as in those days channel steamers had no transportation arrangement for felines. On the world's biggest ship, the Majestic his ticket cost a pound—First Class, of course—and he ate at least four pounds' worth of squab, caviar, charlotte russe and ice cream on the voyage. However this never went to his head, even if it might have at times gone to his tummy. He gave a press conference as the Majestic docked in New York harbour, where a journalist called Zoe Beckley described him as 'a jet-black, fat-jowelled, steady-eyed tomcat', who proved that he hadn't forgotten his humble beginnings by nesting on an old sweater in the corner of Gordon Conway's cabin. 'This shows,' wrote the lady, that he was 'a regular guy and not a silly petted hothouse flower with a lot of satin-quilted baskets and travelling valises!'

Billy—sorry, Mr. Fing—took daily dips in the swimming pools of the international set he now mixed with and attended rehearsals and performances even, in 1921 of *London, Paris and New York*, Dorothy Dickson's first London show. He was in almost daily attendance at most of the West End Theatres, besides appearing at fittings with stars like Jessie Matthews, Evelyn Laye, Hermione Baddeley and Florence Desmond, for whom Gordon Conway designed costumes for plays and films.

But all good things come to an end—even poor Mr. Fing's wonderful, not to say incredible, life—and he died on April 7 1934, aged

13. Gordon Conway and her mother went into deep mourning at their home in Bryanston Court and the cat's ashes were eventually buried in a marble urn under a corner of the Conway family vault at Mount Sion, Caroline County, Virginia, USA. I'd say that Billy-Fing, like Anna Neagle's Tuppence, was stage-struck in a big way, and I'm glad that with all that he never got silly. Even at his peak, with thé dansants at Claridge's, dinner at the Dorchester and dancing at the Savoy, weekends with Dorothy Dickson and 'Little Dot' Hyson at his mistress's country place at Bushey Grange, he still kept going back to see his old friend and discoverer, the proprietor of the Chantecler in Dean Street.

THE WALTZING CAT

Joan Wallace, the opera singer and author, winner of the Nottingham Writer's Club Writer of the Year Award no less than three times, wrote to tell me the lovely story about her dancing cat, Kim, now 23.

Kim, a black as jet alley cat was brought to me by a friend who told me that the little kitten was a runt and didn't have much chance of surviving. To begin with I fed the little thing on chicken-breast, grilled plaice and cream. She has now been with me for 23 years—not bad for a runt with little chance of survival.

Kim loves to waltz. I discovered this one morning about 12 years ago whilst in the middle of putting my make-up on before setting off to work. I was standing in front of the mirror, my make-up spread out on the sideboard and Kim leapt from a chair up on to the sideboard, and commenced scattering my make-up things all over the place. I picked her up in my arms and said 'Naughty little thing,' or something similar, and because there was a waltz playing on the radio, danced round the room with her.

Kim put her arms round my neck, purred like mad, closed her eyes in ecstasy, and when I stopped whirling her round dug her claws into me as though telling me she didn't want me to stop. The following morning Kim once again attacked my make-up until I had swept her up into my arms and danced with her. The peculiar thing was, once she had danced, she was quite satisfied to go to her cushion and settle down—as though she was saying, all right, you can carry on getting ready for work now.

This continued to happen every single morning before I went off to work: the girls I worked with always asked if I'd had a dance with the cat this morning. Sadly, Kim very seldom leaps on to sideboards nowadays because of her rheumatism, but she still enjoys a nice waltz in my arms.

This story reminds me of Furry Wee who used to adore being waltzed around in my arms: it started when I was wearing a blue nightie, and so became 'The Blue Negligée waltz'!

THE SONG OF MEHITABEL

Eileen Atkins has plans for us to dramatize this poem by Don Marquis. It is written by Archy, a cockroach who writes free verse on an office typewriter; Mehitabel is an alley cat.

this is the song of mehitabel
   of mehitabel the alley cat
as i wrote you before boss
   mehitabel is a believer
in the pythagorean
   theory of the transmigration
of the souls and she claims
   that formerly her spirit
was incarnated in the body
   of cleopatra
that was a long time ago
   and one must not be
surprised if mehitabel
   has forgotten some of her
more regal habits

i have had my ups and downs
   but wotthehell wotthehell
yesterday sceptres and crowns
   fried oysters and velvet gowns
and today i herd with bums
   but wotthehell wotthehell

i wake the world from sleep
   as i caper and sing and leap
when i sing my wild free tune
   wotthehell wotthehell
under the blear eyed moon
   i am pelted with cast off shoon
but wotthehell wotthehell

i once was an innocent kit
   wotthehell wotthehell
with a ribbon my neck to fit
   and bells tied onto it
o wotthehell wotthehell
   but a maltese cat came by
with a come hither look in his eye
   and a song that soared to the sky
and wotthehell wotthehell
   and it followed adown the street
the pad of his rhythmical feet
   o permit me again to repeat
wotthehell wotthehell

my youth i shall never forget
   but there s nothing i really regret
wotthehell wotthehell
   there s a dance in the old dame yet
toujours gai toujours gai

the things that i had not ought to
   i do because i ve gotto
wotthehell wotthehell
   and i end with my favourite motto
toujours gai toujours gai

boss sometimes i think
   that our friend mehitabel
is a trifle too gay
                          archy

Eileen with Archie

Eileen thinks that Mehitabel speaks like me. What a lovely thought? Does she, though? Well, I do try to be *Toujours gai, kid, toujours gai.*

AS ONE CAT TO ANOTHER

Valerie Braithwaite wrote this poem to
celebrate playing *Dick Whittington*.

It's pantomime time and once again
   The role I'm to play is very plain.
I'm Dick Whittington and his faithful Cat—
   I'm the one that kills the bad King Rat.

I befriend young Dick and take first prize
   For killing rats that are twice my size,
And to show the Crew what I can do
   I'll need a photograph or two.

So donning Cat-Skin and wide Cheshire grin
I set off to get a few taken.
   On turning the bend
   I bump into a friend
And the sight of me leaves him quite shaken.

Explaining my dress, and with words to
impress
I boast of the part I'm to play;
   The land will be free
   Of all rats—killed by me—
To make everything end quite happily.

My friend is amused at hearing the news
And thinks it a joke from the start;
   He says 'Surely, it's true,
   I'm more cat-like than you
So why shouldn't I get the part?'

Then with eyes all aglare he gives me a stare
And says with a sarcastic mew
   'If a diet of rat
   can make you fat
I'll get in a pantomine too.'

I say with a grin, 'You would never get in—
Just a word before trying too hard;
   You may be a cat,
   and a ratter at that,
But YOU don't have an Equity Card.'

*'A cat may look at an Equity Card
Holder' : Valerie Braithwaite's Puss
confronted by the Real Thing*

THE CAT THAT TALKED

I was amused to hear the following cat story from Roger Carne the ventriloquist, with whom I worked many times when Cuppy the Cat was just a kitten, and to hear again about George Formby, with whom I played the variety theatres and even made my first film appearance when I was just starting out on my career. It was called *Spare A Copper* and often turns up on TV. Try and spot me, terribly thin and singing a sort of soprano song, wearing pince-nez glasses! Roger likes to pull a few legs and spin a few yarns:

I went with the George Formby show on a coast to coast tour of Canada in 1950 and before boarding the ship at Liverpool we passed through customs. The officer said, 'There is a letter for you, Mr. Carne, addressed to Roger Carne and his Cat, c/o the Liner Empress of France, Liverpool. Where is the cat?' I said, 'It's in the bag; I'm taking it to my cabin.'

He said, 'I'm afraid you cannot do that—no animals are allowed in the cabins; it will have to go into the kennels provided aboard ship.' I said 'It will be all right in my cabin and I might want to use it in cabaret on the voyage.' 'Oh no, Sir,' he said, 'the rules are no animals in the cabins.' I said 'But this is a ventriloquist's cat,' to which he replied, 'I don't care if it's Dick Whittington's Cat, it will have to go in the kennels, where the galley boys will look after it and feed it.' I puzzled him even further by saying 'Oh, it doesn't eat.' At that moment George Formby, next in line at the customs, chimed in with, 'It's a talking cat,' which reduced the officer to baffled fury. 'Eeh, lad,' said George Formby, 'it's a dummy cat and he's a ventriloquist: he throws his voice into the cat, and instead of miaowing it talks.'

In the end the officer saw the funny side and Roger was allowed to take Canasta into the cabin with him. It sounds like a scene from one of George Formby's films, and I wonder if Beryl his wife found it funny. She was not exactly famous for her sense of humour, especially when somebody else was getting the laugh!

Cats Around The Honeypot Today

At home, in that lovely stage between sleeping and waking, I can always tell which head is being pushed under my hand by the force behind the head. This is because they think it's stroking time. Tufnell has by far the strongest head, Paris the softest coat, Elsie climbs up on the pillow to sit on top of my head, Ronnie licks my arm and Dimly takes the bull by the horns and jumps on me from the top of the TV set, then he tickles my face with his whiskers and I've got to get up. The others, however, refuse to move till I'm dishing out breakfast and show no interest whatever before the food arrives—then it's everyone for himself.

THE GINGERS

At the moment I'm very lucky indeed because I now have ten cats round the Honeypot—five of them gingers. The eldest one is called Ronnie, after Ronnie Corbett. I found him in a barn at a farm we worked at on location for the film *No Sex, Please—We're British*, which starred Ronnie Corbett. On this farm there was a little black and white cat who used to round up the cows by nipping their heels and getting them in at milking time, which was something I'd never seen in my life and don't think I ever will again. To the critic who took leave to doubt this I have to say it really did happen and I've a whole film crew to prove it. Of course, it's usually a dog that farmers have to round up animals as big as the cows, but they really were very very obedient to the cat, who must have had a very strong personality, and I suspect, a very strong sort of nip on the heels for them. I never found out the cat's name but I always think of it as the 'cat rustler'.

RONNIE

Ronnie the kitten was about three weeks old and had been abandoned by his mother at this farm. He was dying of cat 'flu, and because I was working with some pigs on the film there was a vet on the location. 'I can't leave him here,' I told the vet, 'I must take him home and *try* and do something for him.' The vet replied, 'Well, he won't live, but I'll give him an injection.' Of course there was nowhere really to inject, except the back of his neck, because he was a little tiny scrap, with all this horrid stuff coming out of his nose and his eyes, as always happens with cat 'flu. 'I'll give you nine pills, Beryl,' he told me, 'and keep him away from all your other cats.'

So into the spare room he went with a tin tray and this little round bottle with the nine pills in, which was his one toy, because he wasn't really well enough to play a great deal at that time. That was in 1973, and he's still with me, I think he possibly is on borrowed time, but he has good days and bad days, like everybody does.

At one time he did become very nervous. I had invited five people to lunch and had him in my arms when I opened the door for them to come in. Just at that moment a horse chestnut tree collapsed and went straight through all the overhead electric cables and made this terrible flash, which of course, he from then on associated with people. So for a time he was rather neurotic, but he's quite got over that now, and it's only if he's not feeling very well that he avoids people. And I don't blame him, because I would do exactly the same thing.

People say that cats are very independent. I don't believe this at all, because whenever my car comes home, be it from a day of working on television, or on a film or from a very late night at the theatre, they come out from everywhere: they appear from behind trees—I never arrive home alone. Ronnie walks in front of the car and all I can see is his tail in front of the headlights: he wags it gently from side to side, almost to give me a pointer as to how to get home—as if I didn't know. They are all there and they are all longing to come in: it's a greeting that people who own dogs expect, but of course a lot of barking goes with that. This is a silent greeting, but no less appreciated.

CLIVE AND BILLY

The next two ginger cats that I acquired, also under very unhappy circumstances, are improving They lived under the bed in the spare room for about three months and I could only watch them eat if I looked through the

What again!

window. You see, they had lived in a kennel, and the dog worried them and children threw stones at them and they were absolutely terrified of people. I got them from the RSPCA. They still are very nervous—though not of me; Billy takes frequent trips to the loo with me—he likes it in there and does a great big roll-over, and Clive, is a long-haired, very dark ginger cat, with the most magnificent tail. Sometimes I think he's a fox in the garden, and as mine sit with the foxes it's rather hard to decide which is which. He really is a wonderful cat with a beautiful face and I named him after Clive Francis, with whom I did a season in *The School For Scandal*. If that sounds like a compliment to Clive the man, well, it is. Billy is named after my dear good friend Billy Chappell.

PARIS AND TUFNELL

Then, of course, I had the opportunity of again getting twin brothers from the RSPCA, where Muriel Carey, one of the kindest and most generous people I know, let me have, several lovely cats over the years, about whom more later, except to say that one is named Muriel after her. These twin red heads are the youngest, at this moment ten months old. I must say that they weigh a ton—I don't know how they've got so big in that time. Some cats are heavy and some are light and dainty, but these two are like elephants.

The darker one is called Paris, who is named after the God of Love, and I was thinking of a suitable name for his little brother when I happened to play the record that Irene Handl did with Peter Sellers called *Swinging Sellers* for which she wrote a very funny sketch called 'Shadows On The Grass', which she performed with Peter. I'm a great fan of hers and never tire of hearing this sketch. She refers to her husband, Tufnell, in this way: 'Tufnell left me amply well provided for; I mean, I could purchase any residence I cared to. Tufnell went crackers about me in anything blue, and do you know what he used to call me?—"Squidgy". He said, "Squidgy, buy yourself a blue nightie—make your eyes look like stars!" So, of course, Paris's brother had to be called Tufnell. I've got two Great Lovers in my household!

On the subject of my ginger cats, I feel that Paris, one my twin babies, cannot go unnoticed, because he's so very beautiful. He's very dark ginger with a tiny white spot under his chin and has the most glorious amber eyes that you could ever imagine. He's shy—much shyer than Tufnell, who sucks my nightdress constantly. I call him a 'Succalini' and I said the other day I thought he ought to be in a pram outside Woolworth's with a dummy in his mouth, because I'm sick of him scratching my chest and sucking my nightdress—he really ought to be a little more advanced than that at his age. But, back to Paris, he's really a lovely cat, though slightly shy, so not everyone who comes here has the benefit of his companionship. He does feel a little backward at coming forward, , which, of course, Tufnell doesn't. But with twins there have to be contrasts in personality and Paris is by far the shyer one.

ELSIE

Billy and Clive came to me in 1982. The tortoiseshell cat, now so happily a part of our lives, goes back to three years before that, when I did *Born in the Gardens*, written by Peter Nichols. We opened at the Bristol Old Vic and it was, to my mind, a very very funny play. Jan Waters was in it when it got to London the next year, and she, Peter Bowles and Barry Foster were all my children. My husband had died when the curtain rises, and they've all come to be present at the 'cortaige' as Maud calls it.

I played Maud, and there was a cat called Elsie that belonged to the son played by Barry Foster that we used to talk about. The two characters used to have marvellous drinks. He

— Clive hogging it

Dimly and Tufnell, the greatest of friends

father was a Sikh and their mother a German radiologist, a highly intelligent woman, but obviously not quite used to cats. I asked her 'What's your dear little cat's name?' 'Puzzy' she replied, so I said, 'Well that must have taken a long time to think out! Anyway, I think she's a beautiful little cat.' I used to keep a saucer in my car, on which B. Reid was written in nail varnish and I fed her behind a lot of

She hid from everything and everybody, because she'd got 'people poisoning'.

railings where she used to hide every night. She hid from everything and everybody, because, like Ronnie, she'd got 'people poisoning'.

I kept a tin of cat food and I used to feed her on the way home, and, if nobody was watching, on the way to the theatre. I told the German lady, 'I think she's so beautiful—I would love to take her home with me,' and I showed her pictures of my cats in the garden, and how happy they were and how enormous they were compared to this little thing. The lady said, 'Oh, she is so dirty—she is always makin' a mess in my house in front of my friends and she has ruined the carpet.' Of course, when I got into the house, there was no carpet, and I doubt whether there were friends, but there was a very big colour television and a very big fridge freezer, two items which figured largely in Maud's house in the play.

*Jenny and Elsie and catnip sock.
Who will win?*

would say 'What would you like to drink? Would you like a sloe gin and Campari? You enjoyed that crème de menthe with your haddock.' 'I suppose you gave your haddock to Elsie?' she said. 'Well, only the skin,' he replied. 'That's a bit more like it!' she said.

As time went by in Bristol I acquired a little tortoiseshell cat whom I thought was being quite maltreated. She was a scrappy little thing. There were three Indian children—their

Both Maud and her son used the cat Elsie in the play as an excuse to get across what they wanted to say to each other. The son lived a kind of dream life, entirely tied up with the past, and Maud used to say, 'That cat Elsie lives in the past: she still thinks Dingles is Bright's (referring to a large department store in Bristol). When he wanted to complain about Maud's cooking he would say, 'It's just that Elsie's been grumbling!' I doubt that the German lady's poor little cat figured enough in her life to be referred to in conversation at all, except when I called.

However she did not let her go at all willingly, 'My little girl doesn't want to part with her,' she said, and I replied, 'Then your little girl should treat her better.' In the end I did persuade her, but it took some doing. I gave the children bendy bunnies, which I thought were much more suitable for them to play with, and eventually, between us we managed to get Puzzy into a cat basket, which was difficult, because she was so frightened of people.

Some friends of mine in Bristol, Anne Jeffreys and Nita Hendy, looked after her while I did a matinée and an evening show at the Theatre Royal. She was quite good when she was with them, walking about the kitchen, and then I took her back to Honeypot. She cried all the way in the car, from Bristol to Wraysbury and I was almost demented by the time I got her home.

I put her in the spare room, but, of course, she'd never seen a mirror, and spent a very long time hissing at her own reflection. Poor little thing had never seen anything and she was an absolute hell-cat—only through fear. Naturally, because of her background, Puzzy had become Elsie. Whenever I used to go in to feed her or to put the radio on for her or anything, she flew at my legs. My legs were sort of torn to shreds and I got pretty fed up after three months, because my patience does tend to get exhausted after three months.

Like Hitler my patience was exhausted and I spoke to her in a very sharp voice, 'How do you fancy a one-way trip to the vet, Elsie?' Her whole personality changed from that day to this and she is now one of the most beautiful tortoiseshell cats you've ever seen, she's clean and lovely, whereas before she was covered in oil and grime because she lived under cars, and was ill fed. She behaves really perfectly and at last she's learned to be a kitten. Now she plays with her tail and does all the things that she should have done when she was much younger, but obviously didn't have the opportunity to.

LULU

Lulu came to me as a strange bundle. A lady rang me up from Reading to say that for two years they had tried to capture this wild cat with such a beautiful face. She was living with a vicar's wife, who obviously knew nothing about cats, because she said, 'She seems rather nervous, because I have four very big dogs.' Of course, she would have been frightened out of her life by four very big dogs.

Lulu had had a horrendous life: her tail had been chopped off by some Chinese people (she had a little stump for a tail) and she'd also

Darling Lulu on my roof

not surprised,' I replied, 'Because she's having a fit: at the moment she's unconscious.'

I kept Lulu in the spare room where all the little new ones go for seven months—if they are in that room they have everything they want, including the radio, because I think cats need entertaining. *She* didn't actually live in that room for seven months. About half way through the period I opened the door of the spare room and she used to sit on a chair in the bathroom, which is next door and sort of stare into space. She was exceedingly timid; I think her past life had had a terrible effect on her brain.

The cat flap was right next to the chair in which she sat, and one day there was no Lulu. That was a tremendous grief to me, because I had spent so much time and patience on her, because I realized that she was one of the poorer creatures. And then suddenly she appeared on the roof of my house, where she lived for four years.

This pleased me, except that it caused me to expend a great deal of energy, climbing on to the roof via a step-ladder four times a day

> *I climbed on to the roof via a step-ladder four times a day to feed her for four years.*

watched her kittens being beaten to death. Being a street cat in Reading she soon became pregnant again but her babies died inside her. She had been trapped with one of those cat nets they use to round up strays, and she was whipped to the vet's to remove the dead kittens, but she had never really recovered from the shock of her life.

When this vicar's wife arrived, with a perfectly good cat basket with a little wire cage in the front, she'd hammered wooden slats down the front. I didn't understand this and found it the most heart-rending thing, because if the cat can see where it's going in the car, and you're talking to it, it's not nearly so frightened as if it's shut off from the world.

In fact, when Lulu arrived she was having a fit and foaming at the mouth, and I picked her up. 'This is the first time anybody's been able to pick her up,' said the vicar's wife. 'I'm

to feed her for four years. But I had the consolation that at least Lulu, who had shown me that she didn't want to live inside and preferred to be outside, where she was 'born free', had the comfort of my fire and my chimney, because she used to sleep against it.

So for four years I willingly made the four-times-daily pilgrimage up the ladder.

When the neighbours cut their pine trees down, I realized that she no longer had any way of getting on to the roof. She went missing for about three days. I rang a friend of mine in the Forestry Commission to build a little ladder for her out of a willow tree and add rungs so that she would find it very easy to get up. Because she was slightly dotty from all the terrible earlier experiences of her life (she wouldn't let anybody touch her, or anything), she had forgotten about the roof by the time I had the ladder made and decided she wanted to live on the other side of my stream!

I then went up the stream and collected lumps of concrete and planks and things that I acquired from anybody who had them to supply, and I built her a bridge over to the other side, which I called the Bridge On The River Kwai. She lived somewhere near the boatyard, but every time we found out where she lived she moved again. Obviously she didn't like anyone to know where she lived—there are people like this, not just cats—Lulu was a law unto herself.

She did have five happy years here, and she would let me touch her, pick her up and take all the knots out of her fur (she was a long-haired cat, black with a most beautiful face, and she would go to anyone, eventually, nipping over the bridge quite smartly and letting all my friends feed her.

Then suddenly she went missing again and I couldn't understand this. Obviously she was going to die as she had come to the end of her life. My friend Kim Tracey, who is a clairvoyant and knows my territory said, 'She is sitting in very long grass and she's terribly unhappy. Do go and look for her because I think she is in distress.' Indeed she was when Chris and I managed to find her. Chris drove her to the vet for me in her basket and she died in the arms of one of the nurses or junior veterinary surgeons at the vet's. Lulu's survival—and I'm not giving myself a pat on the back by saying this—was due absolutely to my patience and perseverence because nobody else that I can think of would have bothered. But she was so rewarding and so affectionate when she let me get near her that I felt that I had been repaid a hundredfold.

SIR HARRY, DIMLY AND MURIEL

Muriel Carey, my special friend from the RSPCA, knows better than anyone how much satisfaction there can be in looking after a cat until at last it responds and adjusts to its own kind of happy life. She wrote in the organisation's annual:

'It is always rewarding to hear that our animals have settled in their new homes, but we do get a few awkward cases. One of my most difficult cats to rehome was a white long-haired male who had suffered neglect. He had a mind of his own and a 'nobody loves me' attitude. He was deaf but he had the loudest howl you have ever heard. At meal times he would end up with a bowl of food all over his face and refuse to wash himself. We called him Snoopy and he was with us for quite some time until the day that a very nice couple came to choose a cat and were interested in him. I told them all the drawbacks and problems, but they wanted to give him a home and I was sure they'd give him every chance. Some weeks later I received a card:

Dear Mum, Dad, old friends and anyone else who misses me.

My new Mummy has been trying to phone you to tell you that I am very happy here—so much so that I condescended to wash my right paw last week: might do it again around Christmas; seems to cause a lot of interest.

Food's not up to much, but I reckon if I sit silently by my bowl for days on end refusing what's in it they might get it right in the end. Things are still very quiet as they were at home and I get a lot of fuss made of me and I like that.

There's a lovely pale grey lady puss two doors away who lets me share her garden—much better than that ginger thing at your place. Give him a kiss from me.
Bestest love, Lucifer—né Snoopy.

One day I telephoned Muriel Carey and said, 'I'm getting a little bit short on boys!' Cat Boys, because I seemed to have an awful lot of girls, and at that time very few boys. She said, 'Oh, I've got two *beautiful* kittens in a little litter here. John and I will bring them to see you.' Of course one of them was Sir Harry, who was going to be a very stately, marvellously marked tabby but in the beginning he was very backward. I used to ring Harry Secombe up—he was named after him, naturally—and once I

Sir Harry, with love to the other Sir Harry

told him, 'Harry, he keeps coming in and going to sleep.' 'So did I!' he said. 'But he's so skinny and he doesn't eat anything and he's a nuisance,' I said. 'Yes, so was I—I was all those things.' Harry wouldn't have a word said against that cat.

The other kitten was Dimly, who was quite easy to distinguish. In fact, he grew to

* Dimly, the star

Muriel guarding the bridge

be the biggest while they were growing up. But, in the middle of this lot was a kind of lump of fur and I said, 'What's *that*?', rather like Eileen Atkins' family when, she produced a cat at her father's funeral. 'Well,' they said, 'There are actually three in the litter and we feel we can't separate them.' 'No, I quite agree, but I'll have to speak to Chris about it, to see if she could look after three extra cats.'

So the next day I approached Chris, 'John and Muriel were supposed to bring two boys for me, but three arrived and the middle one was a girl.' Muriel is an old English tortoiseshell, which is quite an unusual breed of cat. She's long-haired and looked like a koala bear when she was little, but the actual thoroughbreds have a coloured mark going through all their four feet, and those who are not thoroughbred have one black foot. Of course, Muriel has got one black foot. Their mother, whom Chris now possesses—she's called Penny—is a through and through pure breed with four feet with light marks going through the middle of them.

With Chris's permission, I took these three in, and, of course, they were a sensational little mob, each having very distinctive personalities. I still think Muriel—the cat namesake—is going to turn into a sheep: she has got so big I don't know what to do with her. Sir Harry has strange habits: he loves noise and children, so when he first went missing—it's easy to go missing here, because it's absolutely countrified—a woman rang me up and said 'Could it be your cat who comes to play every day with my little boy?' She went on 'He's a beautiful little tabby cat.' I asked her 'Do the marks on him make an "O" in the middle? He's "Harry O".' 'Oh yes, they do,' she said. 'Oh, then, I'll come and get him.' She went on, 'I thought I ought to ring you because we're going to move shortly and if he comes every day to look for my little boy he may get lost.' He'd been playing there all day—loved all the noise and kicking about and twigs and all those sort of games that they like if they're gregarious cats like Footy. He loved noisy children and playing about in the garden with them.

When this lady and her son moved, Sir Harry shacked up with a pop group who live at what's called The Big House—the hunting lodge. Of course he sat in with the group,

obviously enjoying the sound of it. Now he doesn't go there any more, but I've found another house that he goes to, and I went along calling frantically for him on one of the occasions when he went missing, and fell over and broke my ribs because I stumbled over a Sleeping Policeman—you know, those lumpy ridges in the road. I was looking up into the sky and not at the ground, and I should have been paying more attention. My friend Olivia Ward says, 'You never look below your bosom, that's why you fall over a lot!'—and I suppose there's a great deal of truth in that.

I went looking for Sir Harry and I asked some people who live just down the lane from me, Mr. and Mrs. Wiseman and their daughter, who have turned out to be absolutely charming, not to feed him—they've promised me that and they always phone me if they think he's been too long with them—'Did I stay too long at the Fair?'! They go to work very early in the morning, about 6.45, and he can nip in there before he comes to me if he's doing a bit of night owling.

When I first went looking for him in that direction—their house is right on the water, you see—I asked them if they'd seen my tabby cat. 'Oh, you mean Tiddles,' she said. 'No, actually its name is Sir Harry!' I replied. 'Oh, he *is* naughty, she said, 'He's had all the cream off the stawberries tonight!' He was less disciplined when he was younger, but now he does have little trips to see them, and we always contact each other, because we have become firm friends through Sir Harry. Since then he has developed into a beautiful cat with a totally different character from the other two. He's out a great deal but always comes back—it would appear that I'm just good digs near wherever he chooses to shack up. If I think he's lost I ring the Wisemans, his latest and dearest friends, and say, 'Have you got Sir Harry?'

Dimly—well, what can I say? Dimly he's not, because he's Brightly: I must have given him quite the wrong name in the beginning. But it was only because Olivia and Terry were staying here and Terry, who is Olivia's husband, said, 'I haven't seen Beryl for quite a long time this morning.' Olivia looked across the little courtyard I've got here—it's a little car-port actually—and said, 'I can just see her moving dimly.' I had to have something called

When I get back from the theatre at twelve or half-past twelve at night I still have to steel myself to roll up a bit of Bacofoil and have a game with him.

Dimly to move, so that's how he got his name, quite unsuitably, as it turned out.

When I get back from the theatre at twelve or half-past twelve at night I still have to steel myself to roll up a bit of Bacofoil and have a game with him. He used to retrieve it like a dog and drop it at my feet, but he's got out of that habit now. He's still most affectionate and adorable, although I am not allowed to have favourites.

WATER BABIES

Dimly, like them all, has his little ways—some of them quite unexpected. One day when I was paying an urgent visit to the loo—like Kath and the 'urgent knitting' she had to do in *Entertaining Mr. Sloane*—I was absolutely rushing, but he beat me to it by about two seconds, and shot under me as I was about to sit down, and, of course, almost got concussion, because he went crashing to the bottom of the basin of the loo and raised a big lump on his head. He was extremely heavy to lift out, because he'd swallowed a great deal of water.

I wondered how on earth I was going to get all the water out of him? If you've got a person, you lie them on their front and press at regular intervals on their back, with both the arms straight. I learnt this when I did a life-saving course when I was about twelve but you can hardly do that with a cat. I thought the only thing to do was to squeeze his ribs, so I kept doing that—'One, two'—and all this water shot out of his mouth like a little fountain in the middle of Trafalgar Square or somewhere.

I dried him and wrapped him in a towel and he slept for about twenty-four hours—he was really rather knocked out by that experience. But, mind you, he has a great fascination for water, or water has a great fascination for him, like it did for Mr. Fing or Billy. Once, when the river was very high the stream was flooded and there were several great big logs of willow trees floating down the stream, I looked out and I couldn't believe my eyes, because there he was, astride one of these willow branches, with a front leg on each side and a back leg on each side, paddling his own canoe. The next time I looked it had turned over, so he was underneath the willow log, and I just walked away. I thought I really can't be involved with this any more—it was so muddy and slippery. I thought he's got in and he'll get out, and, of course he did. The next thing I saw he was nipping smartly across the grass, sopping wet and delighted with himself.

He's really rather thoughtful about water, because when he captured a moorhen—happily he didn't kill it—he put it in the bath for me, which I thought was rather novel; he must have thought that was really where it belonged. Water is bound to figure largely in our lives, because of Honeypot's position right on the Thames edge.

When Ronnie was very little I saw him climbing up my willow tree that has had to be cultivated to hang over the river, because it isn't a weeping willow and it's a wonderful shape now. It's rooted in the river, and the little coots and things find ideal places for nests in it. Anyway, Ronnie shinned up this tree, and I again in my nightdress—it must sound as if that's my permanent state of attire, but it isn't really—nipped smartly into the river and waded out like Silvana Mangano in *Bitter Rice*, because I heard a splash and I was sure it was him. I waded about the river with my night-

dress up to my waist, much to the horror of the fishermen on the opposite bank (perhaps they were riveted by the sight, I don't know) but I got sort of desperate, because I couldn't find a little ginger thing struggling for life in the water. Then, of course, like a fool I looked up into the tree and there he was smiling down at me, Cheshire Cat-like, or like Patience on a monument, smiling at grief.

JENNY

After my lovely cat Emma had died—she managed a very happy existence to the end, quite adjusted to having only one eye—Muriel from the RSPCA told me there was a sweet little tabby who looked so like Emma, that I felt I must at least give her an innings here. Unfortunately, she had belonged to one old lady and had become a one-person cat, and obviously had been allowed to sleep on the old lady's bed or knee, or whatever, and she has found it extremely difficult fitting into a big family like mine is.

Jenny, named after Jenny Agutter, a lovely girl with whom I played at the National Theatre in *Spring Awakening*, is terrified of Dimly and I'm afraid there are a lot of squabbles. He knows that and plays it up wildly, wanting to be the Sylvester Stallone of the cat world, and she squeals even before he has got near her, so I hear these terrible cat noises, I have a pair of very soft slippers that get slung at them during the night, should these things occur. They don't hurt anyone, but they break up the row that is going on and I hear Jenny

Jenny, who finds it hard to fit into a big family, but I love her just the same.

having terrible squabbles with cats outside. It's not her fault, poor little thing—one person, one cat, is a very difficult situation to deal with, which of course I hadn't realized when I took her over.

She has a lovely home, here I discovered that the old lady had fed her on scraps—they are what she still likes best although none of the rest like them. She has also become used to regular feeding: she likes tinned food, not the red stuff that the others eat.

THE ELEPHANTS' GRAVEYARD

The most extraordinary thing to me is that four completely strange cats have come in here to die. It's like the Elephants' Graveyard, really.

I did know who one of them belonged to and I telephoned the owners and said, 'Your cat's dying in our spare bedroom.' There was another one we did know vaguely, a black and white cat called Whisky, who I think was half stray—we called him Whisky, because we had no idea what his real name was. I got the vet to come because he really was very ill and I didn't know what was wrong with him. The vet put him to sleep but not before the cat had bitten Joan, so Joan, in consequence is the only person I know who has had an anti-tetanus injection from a vet!

There was a cat I'd never seen before who came in and did die in the spare room. Then there was Nikki, who didn't quite make it to the house. He did belong to somebody who, I'm afraid, didn't look after him at all well, and so he used this as a kind of haven as I had given him food for sixteen years. Chris looked out of the window one morning and said, 'Oh, there's a dead cat on the path—don't ask me to go and get it!'—and she's really marvellous with cats. So I went and got him—it was a pelting wet night—and he had died on the path trying to get to the house, because he used to come through the cat flap and sleep in the baskets secretly—the baskets are on the top of wardrobes. He was quite a cheeky fellow but his luck ran out and he had just dropped dead on the path. His owners weren't at all pleased that he hadn't gone to their house to die, but I don't blame him at all, nor do I know what he died from.

I have a most wonderful vet called Brian Woodward and he doesn't come in and stand and look like a vet, which the one I had before used to. I used to say to him, 'Don't stand there looking like a vet,' because all the cats were terrified! Brian is a great big lovely bear of a man and the only thing he gets mixed up is their sexes. But as he'd neutered them all I said, 'I really worry about you and your own life, because if you don't know what sex these are it's a pretty poor look-out!'

Well, there it is. I have learnt so much I didn't know about cats through writing this book and only hope I've been able to communicate some of that knowledge and the pleasure I have felt in writing about my favourite species.

According to Chinese astrology, which features 12 animals in an astrological cycle of years, people born in a Year of the Cat are refined and virtuous, lovers of tradition, discreet, clever, altruistic. That sounds very nice, but on the other hand these same people may also be pedantic, aloof, devious and oversensitive. Not so nice. Apparently you have to leave it all up to the Management.

The last Year of the Cat was 1975: the next is 1987, the year this book will be around. Well, I hope that's a very good omen:

Index

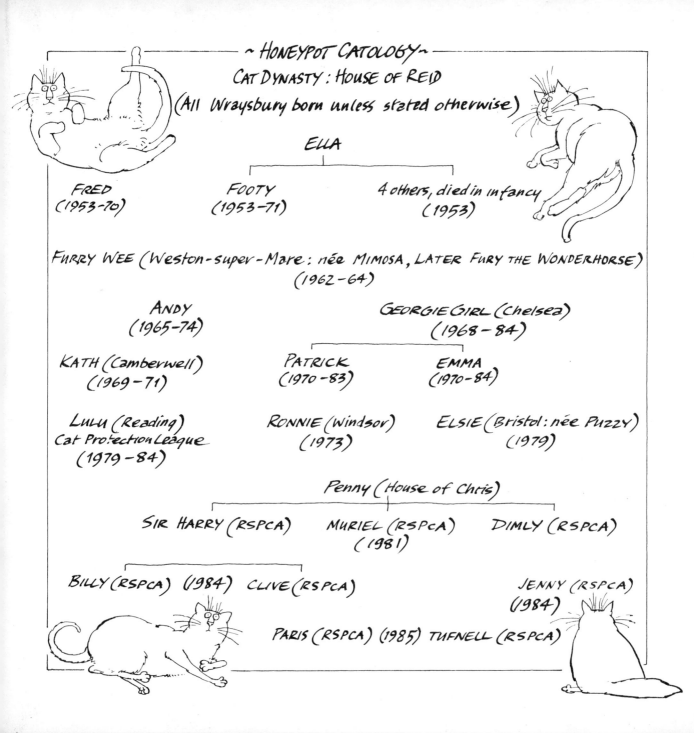

~ HONEYPOT CATOLOGY ~

CAT DYNASTY: HOUSE OF REID

(All Wraysbury born unless stated otherwise)

ELLA

FRED
(1953–70)

FOOTY
(1953–71)

4 others, died in infancy
(1953)

FURRY WEE (Weston-super-Mare: née MIMOSA, LATER FURY THE WONDERHORSE)
(1962–64)

ANDY
(1965–74)

GEORGIE GIRL (Chelsea)
(1968–84)

KATH (Camberwell)
(1969–71)

PATRICK
(1970–83)

EMMA
(1970–84)

LULU (Reading)
Cat Protection League
(1979–84)

RONNIE (Windsor)
(1973)

ELSIE (Bristol: née PUZZY)
(1979)

Penny (House of Chris)

SIR HARRY (RSPCA)

MURIEL (RSPCA)
(1981)

DIMLY (RSPCA)

BILLY (RSPCA) (1984)   CLIVE (RSPCA)

JENNY (RSPCA)
(1984)

PARIS (RSPCA) (1985) TUFNELL (RSPCA)